THE STRUCTURE OF BIOLOGICAL THEORIES

SUNY Series in Philosophy and Biology
David Edward Shaner, Editor
Furman University

THE STRUCTURE OF BIOLOGICAL THEORIES

PAUL THOMPSON

State University of New York Press

Published by
State University of New York Press, Albany

For information, address State University of New York
Press, State University Plaza, Albany, N.Y., 12246

Library of Congress Cataloging in Publication Data

Thompson, Paul, 1947–
        The structure of biological theories / Paul Thompson.
        p.   cm. — (SUNY series in philosophy and biology)
        Bibliography: p.
        ISBN 0-88706-933-9. ISBN 0-88706-934-7 (pbk.)
        1. Evolution.   2. Evolution—Philosophy.   I. Title.   II. Series.
        QH371.T494 1989
        575.01—dc19   88-15376
                                                                    CIP

10   9   8   7   6   5   4   3   2   1

for Jennifer McShane, and
Jonathan, Erinn and Kerry
1   4   3   7

Contents

viii   CONTENTS

Preface

The central thesis of this book is that the semantic conception of theory structure represents more accurately the logical structure of evolutionary theory and provides a richer understanding of the epistemological, methodological, and heuristic features of foundational work in evolutionary biology than does the more widely adhered-to syntactic conception (often called "the received view"). Indeed, I argue that a number of the current controversies in evolutionary biology can be more adequately and accurately understood and satisfactorily resolved on a semantic conception of theories than they can on a syntactic conception.

My intellectual debts which have made the writing of this book possible are many. I am, of course, extremely indebted to John Beatty (a good friend and an excellent philosopher and historian of biology) for his helpful comments and advice, and to Elisabeth Lloyd, who has brought clarity to a number of issues in the philosophy of biology. Both have labored with me in developing and promoting the semantic conception of theory structure as applied to biology. And I am indebted to Bas van Fraassen for comments and support. His writings, along with those of Frederick Suppe, have had an enormous influence on the thesis of this book. Indeed, it was their writings that opened up for me an exciting new way to understand the logic and methodology of foundational work in science and especially foundational work in evolutionary biology. I am also indebted to my colleagues at the University of Toronto for their help, support, and friendship, and especially to Ronald de Sousa, who made numerous very helpful suggestions on an earlier draft.

I also owe a very great debt to two philosophers for whom I have great admiration and respect but whose views I criticize extensively in this book: Michael Ruse and Alexander Rosenberg. Without the clarity and analytic rigor of their presentations and defenses of various aspects of biological theorizing, the field of the philosophy of biology would be very much poorer and my task more difficult if not impossible. It is precisely because their writings brought philosophical rigor to the discussions of the structure of evolutionary theory that I was able to see clearly what I think are the major deficiencies in the dominant understanding of the nature of biological theorizing. In addition, their criticisms of my positions and arguments have helped enormously in forcing me to clarify my thinking and to work out more carefully and fully some aspects of the semantic conception of theory structure that I had quite uncritically and unjustifiably passed over.

I am also very indebted to Wim van der Steen and Peter Sloep for making me painfully aware that although the semantic conception of theory structure may provide a richer understanding of some aspects of biological theorizing, it is not a panacea for all theoretical and conceptual issues in biology, and that, as with the syntactic conception, there are limits to its usefulness as a tool for the philosophical analysis of science.

My debts, as one might expect in an interdisciplinary area, extend to many who are not philosophers by training. Some are biologists whom I know primarily through their writings: Richard Lewontin, Richard Levins, and Ernst Mayr have had an enormous influence on my thinking about evolutionary biology. Some, however, I know through more than their writings. Francisco Ayala, with whom it was my privilege to coteach a philosophy of biology course at the University of California, Davis, enriched my understanding of biological thought, especially with regard to functional analysis and teleology in biology. Ronald Williams has made me stop and rethink my positions and arguments on more occasions than, I suspect, he is aware. And Ronald Brooks and Charles (Pat) McCormack, imparted to me their infectious enthusiasm for the study of animal behavior and circadian rhythms respectively.

One person to whom I owe a great deal is Thomas Goudge. It was his book *The Ascent of Life* which opened up, to a beginning graduate student, the conceptual and theoretical richness of biology at a time when few philosophers thought biology to be of much interest. And it was his encouragement that focused and developed that interest.

It is my hope that this book will provide a systematic treatment of theory structure in biology that will demonstrate the correctness, richness, and heuristic value of the semantic conception of theories in the context of biological theorizing. However, I shall consider the book a success even if it only achieves one of the following: a reinforcement of the value of formalization in biological theorizing; a sowing of the seeds of doubt about the appropriateness of the syntactic conception as an account of theory structure in biology; or a clarification and illustration of the importance of conceptions of theory structure to a wide range of foundational issues in biology. Of course, I shall be most satisfied if it produces substantial numbers of converts to the semantic conception.

Introduction

During the last three decades, philosophers of science have discovered biology to be a rich mine of conceptual, logical, and epistemological issues—at least as rich as physics: I believe richer. Examples of this richness can be found readily in the increasing body of philosophical literature on biology. For example, the richness and complexity of the concept of selection can be seen in Elliott Sober's extremely insightful book in which he discusses the empirical character of the concept of selection, the level at which selection occurs, the causal role of selection, and other matters. An especially compelling example of the conceptual richness of biology can be found in the writings of David Hull on the concept 'species'. Among the important issues he has tackled are whether species are natural kinds or individuals or classes of individuals, and whether species are the entities that evolve.

In this book, I primarily explore the logical, epistemological, and methodological aspects of biological theorizing. I hope that I have shown that biology is also in these respects a rich and complex science. I also hope that I have offered a useful diagnosis of the cause, and a fruitful framework for the resolution, of several difficult and controversial issues in current biological theorizing.

A central tenet of my approach to the structure of biological theories is that formalization is *one* (though by no means the only) important route to understanding science and to making major theoretical advances within science. This point, I think, has been put most succinctly by Patrick Suppes:

> The role of philosophy of science is to clarify conceptual problems and to make explicit the foundational assumptions of each scientific discipline . . . In the context of such clarification and construction, a primary method of philosophical analysis is that of formalizing and axiomatizing the concepts and theories of fundamental importance in a given domain of science. To argue that such formalization is one important method of clarification is not in any sense to claim that it is the only method of philosophical analysis (Suppes 1968, p. 653).

In conformity with this central tenet, this book is about the formalization of biological theories, in particular the theories of evolutionary biology. I hope to have shown the importance of formalization by showing how important conceptual and theoretical problems of evolutionary biology have been incorrectly understood, and how proffered solutions have been inadequate, in large

1

part, because of a widespread adherence to a particular conception of the formal structure of theories—a conception that I refer to as "the syntactic conception." However, what I also hope will be clear from a reading of this book is that even this widely adhered-to view, which I severly criticize, has been of enormous importance to our understanding of biological science and hence serves to support the claimed importance of formalization.

One central issue in the philosophy of biology is the structure of evolutionary theory. Among the numerous accounts of the structure of evolutionary theory are the "syntactic conception" accounts of Michael Ruse, Mary Williams, and Alexander Rosenberg. I have two objections to such "syntactic accounts." First, the general framework within which they construct their views on the logical structure of evolutionary theory is flawed. Moreover, this general framework is not just flawed with regard to formalizing evolutionary theory—it is also flawed as a general approach to theory structure in all contexts. Indeed, the most damaging criticisms of it have come from philosophers interested in theories of physics.

Hilary Putman, Kenneth Schaffner, Frederick Suppe, Patrick Suppes, and Bas van Fraassen, to mention only a few, have all argued that this framework is inadequate as an account of the structure of physical theories. In chapter 2, I set out these criticisms after having examined the logical, epistemological, and methodological aspects of this conception of theory structure. In chapter 3, I set out the syntactic conception accounts of Ruse, Williams, and Rosenberg on the structure of evolutionary theory and argue that although each has captured important aspects of evolutionary theory, none captures its true character as set out in chapter 1. I argue that the cause of this shortcoming can be traced to their adherence to a syntactic conception of theory structure.

My second objection is that adherence to this conception has resulted in philosophers of biology seriously mischaracterizing evolutionary theory and thereby failing to adequately capture and exploit the complexity and richness of the theory and its relationship to other theories. Indeed, many important controversies in biology continue to appear intractable because of this mischaracterization. For example, the exciting prospect of taking seriously the evolutionary component to the nature and acquisition of knowledge has been hindered, I argue, by the overly simple characterization of evolutionary theory and its relationship to phenomena.

This overly simple characterization is, I maintain, in large part the result of constraints placed on formalization within the syntactic conception of theory structure. It has also made it impossible to take seriously the role of culture and culturally transmitted information in a theoretical account of human knowledge and ethics—attempts have been artificial, resulting in distortions. The two general points that emerge from this analysis are that the conception one adopts on theory structure profoundly affects a vast number of, if not all, biological issues, and that the syntactic conception has profound negative effects on the understanding and resolution of numerous biological issues.

I argue that a recently developed conception of theories, called the "semantic conception," which was initially worked out in the context of physics, is more faithful to foundational work in biology and provides a richer framework for understanding the logical, epistemological, and methodological aspects of theorizing in biology. Specifically, it provides a richer framework for understanding and investigating the structure of evolutionary theory, sociobiology, and culture and the evolutionary process. This is the main thesis of the book.

With regard to the plan of the book, in the first chapter I outlined three extremely important and widely discussed foundational issues within evolutionary biology. I set out the nature of the controversy over these issues and indicate the fundamental importance of these issues within evolutionary biology. One of the major goals of the book is to establish that these issues can be better understood and resolved when a semantic, rather than a sytactic, conception of theory strucure is presupposed.

I then provide an account of the dominant syntactic conception of theory structure and some of the variants that have been adopted. This account highlights the central features of this view and develops in a comprehensive way the major (and, I think, fatal) logical, epistemological, and methodological criticisms of this conception. Since much of the material in this chapter requires some familiarity with mathematical logic, formal semantics, and metalogic, I have provided a very brief, nontechnical summary at the end in the hope that those with little or no knowledge in these areas will still find the material in the rest of the book accessible and relevant.

Next, I examine two extremely influential, and very important, attempts to cast evolutionary theory in terms of the syntactic conception of theory structure. One account has been offered by Michael Ruse, and another by Mary Williams and Alexander Rosenberg. These attempts, I argue, provide certain insights into biological theorizing and into the nature of evolutionary theory but are ultimately inadequate. A number of the inadequacies have been set out by Elliott Sober, John Beatty, Richard Lewontin, and me as well as by Ruse and Rosenberg in their criticisms of the alternative account to their own. I discuss these problems and then argue that the fundamental problem with these syntactic accounts is that they assume, and must assume in order for a syntactic account to be possible, that evolutionary theory is a unified theory. Hence each, in order to achieve theoretical unity, equates evolutionary theory with only one of the component theories that constitute an evolutionary theoretical framework, I argue that evolutionary theory is not a unified theory.

Instead, it is, as Morton Beckner insightfully argued three decades ago, a family of interacting theories. And, as such, no syntactic account of the theory can be given.

I move next to a discussion of the semantic conception of theory structure. I provide an account of two versions of this conception: a set theoretical version (as developed by Patrick Suppes) and a state space version (as developed by Bas van Fraassen and Frederick Suppe). As with the account of the syntactic conception, I have provided a very brief, nontechnical summary of the semantic conception in the last section of this chapter. Though brief, this summary, I think, will make the other material and central thesis of the book accessible and relevant to those who have little or no knowledge of set theory, topology, and metalogic.

Having set out both conceptions and provided arguments in support of the inadequacy of the syntactic conception as a general account of theories and as an account of evolutionary theory, I argue in the next three chapters that the semantic conception is a richer account of theorizing in biology. Specifically, I argue that it provides a more faithful account of foundational work in population genetics; it makes possible a formal account of evolutionary theory as a family of interacting theories; it casts a substantial amount of light on the methodological problems that have plagued sociobiology (such as the testability of the theory and the ad hoc character of its explanations); and it provides a richer logical framework for characterizing the more sophisticated and exciting understanding of evolutionary epistemology and evolutionary ethics contained in recent accounts.

On the last of these advantages of the semantic conception, I argue in a programmatic fashion that, on a semantic conception but not on a syntactic conception, one can provide a rich and complex account of the role played in causal explanations of epistemology by biological evolution; learning; and culturally transmitted information, patterns of behavior, and institutions.

CHAPTER 1

Theory Structure and Foundational Issues in Evolutionary Biology

In this chapter I briefly outline three foundational issues in biology to which I return in later chapters: the structure of evolutionary theory, sociobiology, and culture and the evolutionary process. What I argue in later chapters is that one's conception of theory structure has a profound effect on the formulation, discussion, and resolution of debate on each of these issues. Indeed, the discussion of these issues in later chapters constitutes important evidence for the thesis of this book: that a semantic conception of theory structure provides a methodologically richer, more accurate, more conceptually useful, and more logically adequate account of theorizing in biology. By showing that the semantic conception makes possible a methodologically richer and a more adequate account of the theoretical aspects of each of these issues, I will have provided considerable evidence for this central thesis. I also will have indicated the nature of a more general application of the semantic view to other foundational issues and of the advantages that a more general application will bring with it.

I have chosen these three issues for four main reasons. First, they are, and have been over the last decade, the subjects of heated controversy. Second, they are either of fundamental importance to evolutionary biology or are extremely promising enterprises whose promise has been thwarted by significant logical and methodological problems. Third, they illustrate well the major defects of a syntactic conception of theory structure and the enormous virtues of a semantic conception. Fourth, the methodological and logical problems associated with each of these issues are typical of such problems with other foundational issues, and hence they provide an excellent basis for generalization concerning the defects of a syntactic conception of theory structure and the virtues of a semantic conception.

In this chapter I only provide a sketch of these three foundational issues. A more detailed discussion is postponed until after the rival conceptions of theory structure have been discussed. My goal in this chapter is simply to indicate the nature of the controversy surrounding each issue and the significance and interest that it holds within evolutionary biology. In each case I indicate what I take to be the important features of the issue that an adequate

5

conception of theory structure will have to capture. In later chapters I argue that adherence to a syntactic conception of theory structure has resulted in methodological and logical problems because it has led to a misidentification and misrepresentation of the important logical features of a theoretical framework or a distorted explanatory programme within a theoretical framework. More importantly, I also argue that a semantic conception does capture the important features identified in this chapter.

1.1. The Theory of Evolution as a Family of Interacting Models

Although speculation and theorizing about biological evolution occurred prior to the publication of the *Origin of Species* by Charles Darwin in 1859 (see, for example, Lamark 1809 and Chambers 1844), the development of the modern synthetic theory of evolution began with Darwin. And, although it was not until 1858, when the papers of Darwin and Alfred Russel Wallace were read to the Linnaean Society, that the theory was made public, Darwin had been working on it for a considerable length of time and had "discovered" the causal principle of natural selection twenty years earlier in 1838: six years before the publication of *Vestiges* by Chambers.

This discovery of the principle of natural selection is widely held to be the foundational insight and main contribution of Darwin that began the theoretical lineage[1] that has resulted in contemporary evolutionary theorizing. Natural selection is based, for Darwin, on the *struggle for survival*, a term he understood in a "large and metaphorical sense" (Darwin 1968, p. 116). Although Darwin does not explicitly claim that *natural selection* is a metaphor, I take it also to be a metaphor which is intended to suggest that a natural and nonteleological process of culling, analogous to purposeful human culling in animal and plant breeding, takes place in nature and has resulted in evolutionary change. The empirical content of this metaphor has been the subject of considerable debate since Darwin suggested it. Elliott Sober's recent book, *The Nature of Selection (1984b)*, is an excellent treatment of the contemporary issues surrounding the empirical meaning and theoretical role of natural selection in evolutionary theory.

That natural selection as a mechanism of evolutionary change was an important contribution of Darwin is undeniable. However, one has to take care not to elevate its role in a complete theory of evolution. It should not, for example, be elevated to such a position that a theory of natural selection is taken as equivalent to a theory of evolution. This is, in effect, the assumption underlying Mary Williams's axiomatization of evolutionary theory (Williams 1970) and is the explicit position of Alexander Rosenberg (Rosenberg 1985) in his exposition and defense of Williams's axiomatization (see 3.2 above).

Nor should it be elevated to the position of being the major conceptual difference between an evolutionary perspective and a nonevolutionary perspective. The first of the two ways in which the role of natural selection in evolutionary theory should not be overemphasized is the major focus of this section and of sections 3.2 and 5.3. However, I shall briefly discuss the second before turning to the first. The main reasons for discussing the second at all, since I shall not return to it again, are (1) to indicate the extent and danger of expecting more of natural selection within evolutionary theory than it can deliver, and (2) to emphasize the importance of speciation in an adequate definition of evolution.

Natural selection is without a doubt an important mechanism of evolutionary change, and certainly no theory bearing the name *Darwinian* could reasonably have no role for it; the neutralist view of Kimura (1983) is quite properly called "non-Darwinian." Nonetheless, accepting natural selection as a mechanism of change does not make one a Darwinian or an evolutionist. Nor does it alone constitute a complete theory of evolution.

Natural selection should not be understood as the principal *conceptual* difference between an evolutionary perspective and a nonevolutionary perspective because, as Darwin himself recognized, natural selection can only be a causal mechanism of the evolution of new species if species are mutable, and, as indicated below, natural selection does not entail the mutability of species. Hence, the primary conceptual dividing line between an evolutionary perspective and a non-evolutionary perspective is the acceptance that species are mutable. Darwin had become convinced of the mutability of species as early as 1837. In 1844 he wrote to Hooker: "I am almost convinced (quite contrary to the opinion I started with) that species are not (it is like confessing a murder) immutable." And Darwin fully appreciated the importance of this conceptual change to the acceptability of the view he later developed on the truth of evolution as a phenomenon and on the causal mechanisms of evolution:

> Although I am fully convinced of the truth of the views given in this volume under the form of an abstract, I by no means expect to convince experienced naturalists whose minds are stocked with a multitude of facts all viewed, during a long course of years, from a point of view directly opposite to mine. . . . A few naturalists, endowed with much flexibility of mind, and who have already begun to doubt on the immutability of species, may be influenced by this volume; but I look with confidence to the future, to young and rising naturalists, who will be able to view both sides of the question with impartiality. Whoever is led to believe that *species are mutable* will do good service by conscientiously expressing his conviction; *for only thus can the load of prejudice by which this subject is overwhelmed be removed* (Darwin 1968, p. 453; emphasis added)

It is clearly for this reason that Darwin spent such a considerable amount of time in the *Origin* establishing that species were mutable.

> I can entertain no doubt, after the most deliberate study and dispassionate judgement of which I am capable, that the view which most naturalists entertain, and which I formerly entertained—namely, that each species has been independently created—is erroneous. I am fully convinced that species are not immutable; but that those belonging to what are called genera are lineal descendants of some other and generally extinct species, in the same manner as the acknowledged varieties of any one species are the descendants of that species. (Darwin 1968, p. 69)

What, in fact, Darwin argued was that species are not real but are rather the result of a useful but artificial classification of an insensible gradation of organisms. Hence, species are not immutable because they are not real natural entities.

> Certainly no clear line of demarcation has as yet been drawn between species and sub-species—that is, the forms which in the opinion of some naturalists come very near to, but do not quite arrive at the rank of species; or, again, sub-species and well marked varieties and individual differences. These differences blend into each other in an insensible series; and a series impresses the mind with the idea of actual passage. . . . Hence, I believe a well marked variety may be justly called an incipient species; but whether this belief be justifiable must be judged by the general weight of the several facts and views given throughout this work. (Darwin 1968, p. 107)

> From these remarks it will be seen that I look at the term species, as one arbitrarily given for the sake of convenience to a set of individuals closely resembling each other, and that it does not essentially differ from the term variety, which is given to less distinct and more fluctuating forms. The term variety, again, in comparison with mere individual differences, is also applied arbitrarily, and for mere convenience sake. (Darwin 1968, p. 108)

This view of species as a convenient but arbitrary category of the classification of organisms which is based solely on resemblance makes the title *The Origin of Species* somewhat peculiar, as John Beatty has pointed out (Beatty 1983, p. 79; see the commentary on this paper by Hull [in the same volume], who agrees entirely with Beatty).

The essence of the argument that the mutability of species and not natural selection is the primary conceptual difference between an evolutionary and nonevolutionary perspective is as follows. Natural selection acting on variation within a population will not produce evolutionary change in the most important and interesting sense of evolutionary change even if the results of selection have effects on the next generation. It will certainly change the genetic structure of the population and the phenotypic structure of the population. But it will not necessarily produce a new species of organism. And, if one holds that species are immutable, then the mechanisms of 'evolution' cannot produce new species.

Consider the classic peppered moth (*Biston betularia*) example of natural selection. Because of a changing environment (darkening of the tree bark from industrial pollution) the melanic (black) form of the moth became less visible to predators while the white form became more visible. This change resulted in selective pressure against the white form and for the melanic form. The results of this selective pressure were heritable. However, no new species of moth were created and certainly no new kind of organism was produced. All that occurred was an alteration of gene frequencies. Of course, if one believes that species are mutable, then this episode of selection becomes but one step in a series of episodes which, when added up, result in a very different kind of organism. If, however, one does not believe in the mutability of species, then all one has is a number of episodes of change *within* a species. The cumulative product of such episodes cannot, in principle, be a new species.

A number of important points emerge from this characterization of the role of natural selection. The first, which follows directly from what has been said, is that natural selection is not a sufficient condition of speciation. This is not a controversial point: almost all scholars accept that heritability of the selected characteristics and the production of new variations are necessary components of Darwinian evolution. What emerges from the above discussion, however, is that variation, heritability, and selection also are not jointly sufficient conditions for speciation, and, hence, evolution, to occur. Species must also be mutable.

The second point, which has recently been highlighted by Niles Eldredge and Steven J. Gould (see Eldredge and Gould 1972; Gould and Eldredge 1977; Gould 1980a, 1980b, 1981, 1982; Eldredge 1985a, 1985b), is that natural selection is not a necessary condition of speciation either. Although I do not believe that Eldredge and Gould are correct in the claim that *most* species are formed extremely rapidly by genetic, chromosomal, etc., revolutions, it seems undeniable that some species are formed in this way (see Stebbins and Ayala 1981 and Ayala 1983 for very helpful discussions of this controversy). Hence, in some cases natural selection may have played no role at all in the *formation* of a large number of species. Once formed, of course, selection is an operative force which may result in the transformation or rapid extinction of species formed through a genetic revolution. What follows from the view of Eldredge and Gould is that natural selection is not a necessary condition of species *formation*. What is a necessary, though not sufficient, condition of species formation by means of an evolutionary process, however, is the mutability of species. The very possibility of speciation requries that species be mutable. If they are not, speciation (rapid and gradual), and hence evolution, is impossible.

A third point that emerges from the above is that, in defining evolution, species formation must be a principal feature of the definition. It is not necessary that one believe that species are 'real', in the sense of a Platonic form or a natural kind, in order to take seriously the need for any definition of evolution to include reference to the formation of new groups of organisms. Selection which results only in a change in the frequency of existing characteristics within a specified group of organisms is not evolution. Hence, defining evolution in terms of changes in gene frequencies alone is inadequate. The changes in gene frequencies must result in the formation of a new group of organisms. As indicated above, if species are immutable, changes in gene frequencies will not result in evolution. Indeed, evolution is impossible—only special creation or saltational events will result in new groups of organisms. But, even if species are mutable, changes in gene frequencies is not a sufficient, though it is a necessary, condition of evolution.

Evolution, then, must be defined in a way that includes as a necessary condition the requirement that new groups of organisms (natural or artificially specified) be formed. Evolution is not just changes in gene frequencies, nor is it natual selection acting on populations. It is *the formation of new groups of organisms (species) from existing species*. Hence, a theory of evolution must be a description of the causal mechanisms which result in *the formation of new species from existing species*. Of course, the mechanisms of population and molecular genetics will figure prominently among these causal mechanisms (see Ayala and Valentine 1979 and Lewontin 1974).

With this last point in mind, I turn now to a discussion of the first point made above about the role of natural selection in evolutionary theory, namely, that its role in a theory of evolution should not be overemphasized by regarding a theory of natural selection as equivalent to a theory of evolution. This is a quite different point from the one just made. Although natural selection will not result in evolution if species are immutable, it might be, and indeed has been, thought sufficient to do so if species are mutable.

Although Darwin placed great importance on the mechanism of natural selection ("Furthermore, I am convinced that Natural Selection has been the main but not exclusive means of modification": Darwin 1968, p. 69), he was also well aware of the need for some mechanism of heredity ("Any variation which is not inherited is unimportant for us": p. 75) and some mechanism for the generation of variation within populations (see Darwin 1968 chapters 1 and 2). Though aware of their importance, he was unsuccessful, in light of current theories, in his attempts to provide an acceptable account of either heredity or variation.

Assuming, as I shall for the rest of this book, that species are mutable, an adequate Darwinian theory of evolution (i.e., one in which natural selection is a major mechanism) must include mechanisms of heredity and variation. This is, of course, not to suggest that non-Darwinian theories of evolution in which natural selection plays no role are impossible. Quite the contrary, what I and many others have maintained (see Lewontin 1974; Sober 1981) is that selection, heredity, and variation are *jointly sufficient* to produce evolutionary change. Whether they are also individually or jointly *necessary* is an open question to which neutralists have already answered no. The fundamental *logical* requirement of a scientific theory is that its mechanisms in some combination be *sufficient* for the occurrence of the phenomena within its scope, not that they be individually or in some combination *necessary* for the occurrence of the phenomena. When more than one theory describes mechanisms that are *sufficient* for the occurrence of the phenomenon, it is a complex issue as to which explains the actual empirical phenomenon under investigation. In some cases this question is considered resolved by experimentation. In most and probably all cases, however, the issue is sufficiently complex that no simple recourse to experimentation and successful prediction will be decisive. Theory and phenomena are too inextricably interconnected to make any easy determination possible. In practice numerous nonexperimental considerations, such as simplicity, heuristic value, compatibility with other deeply held convictions, relative significance of unresolved problems, and so forth, play a role in one's choice of competing theories. For the purposes of this book I take for granted that a Darwinian theory of evolution which is commonly called "the modern synthetic theory" is the theory of evolution almost universally accepted as the most accurate account of the mechanism of the phenomenon of evolution as it is currently understood.

What I am maintaining, then, is that an adequate Darwinian evolutionary theory (that is, one that describes mechanisms that are sufficient for the occurrence of evolution) must, in addition to describing mechanisms of natural selection, describe mechanisms of heredity and mechanisms of variation. The basis for this claim is that natural selection cannot by itself lead to evolution. All three components are necessary for evolutionary change to occur (selection, heredity, and variation). Without variation there is no possibility of directional selection. Without selection there is no exploitation of variability and hence no *nonrandom* alteration of the phenotype, and consequently of the genetic structure of populations. Though there are other mechanisms of population change (random drift, for example), selection remains of prime importance. However, although selection will alter the phenotypic structure of a population, unless characteristics are heritable there will be no effect of this selection on subsequent generations. Heredity, therefore, is of fundamental importance.

Evolutionary theory is a composite, then, of natural selection, heredity, and variation. The difficulty that this understanding of evolutionary theory poses in connection with a formal account of the theory is that it is not a unified theory. Currently, there exists, at best, a theory of selection in which the mechanisms of ecological theory are included; a theory of heredity which for all practical purposes in the context of evolution can be identified with population genetical theory but in fact also includes molecular genetical theory; and, though far from complete, a theory of variation. Although there are connections between these theoretical frameworks, they are in no sense unified into a single theoretical framework, contrary to what the title of Fisher's famous work (Fisher 1930), *The Genetical Theory of Natural Selection*, might lead one to believe. In Fisher's calculus and in the calculus of modern population genetics, selection is a numerical parameter which is not determined from within the calculus. Indeed, the selection parameter is often a function of events and mechanisms operating at the level of phenotypes and not at the level of events and mechanisms described by population genetics, that is, genotypes (this point is dealt with more extensively in chapter 5).

This latter point suggests another connected layer of complexity. Not only is the theory not a unified theory in the sense that not all the mechanisms are described within a single framework, but the component frameworks describe mechanisms that operate at different levels of organic organization and operate on quite different kinds of entities. It is this fact that caused Richard Lewontin (Lewontin 1974) to claim that evolutionary theory involves at least two different state spaces—a phenotypic and a genotypic state space—and that an adequate evolutionary theory involves tranformation laws that describe the interaction between the two spaces: "It would appear that both genotypes and phenotypes are state variables and that what population genetic theory does is to map a set of genotypes into a set of phenotypes, provide a transformation in the phenotype space, then map these new phenotypes back into genotypes, where a final transformation occurs to produce the genotype array in the next generation" (Lewontin 1974, p. 13).

Diagrammatically, Lewontin's position is as follows:.

In this diagram p_1–p_4 are phenotypes. g_1 g_3 and g_5 are genotypes (zygotes).g_2 and g_4 are sets of gametes. T_2 and T_6 are sets of transformation laws which include laws of mating, migration, selection, etc. They transform a phenotype from one generation to the next. T_1 and T_5 are sets of laws which transform genotypes into phenotypes. These sets will include laws of embryological development. T_3 and T_7 are sets of laws which transform phenotypes into gametes through the process of gamete formation. T_2 and T_4 are sets of laws which transform gametes into zygotes.

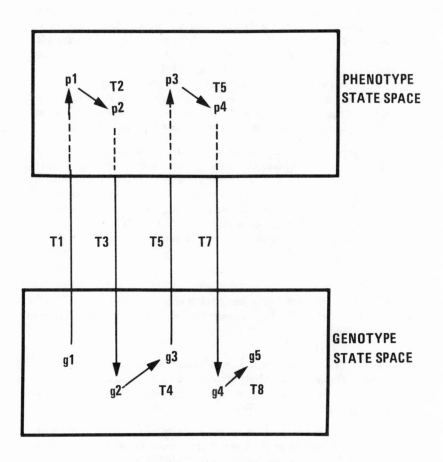

Redrawn from Lewontin 1974, p. 14.

The quotation from Lewontin should not be misunderstood as advocating the primacy of population genetic theory. Lewontin is outlining, in this passage, what must be *taken into account* within population genetic theory and not what is strictly speaking genotypic in nature or determined genotypically. As he makes clear in other passages, the transformation laws that map phenotypes into phenotypes within the phenotype space are phenotypic and not genotypic:

> In equation (1) [$\Delta q = (q(1-q)/2)(d \ln \bar{w}/dq)$] these pseudoparameters are the fitnesses associated with the individual genotypes in computing the function $\bar{w}$. Fitness, however, is a function of the phenotype, not the genotype, al-

though in special circumstances it might turn out that a one-to-one constant correspondence existed between genotype and fitness. More usually, however, relative fitnesses of phenotypes will be a function of the phenotype composition of the population as a whole, so that fitnesses assigned to genotypes in each generation will themselves follow a law of transformation that depends upon the genotype-phenotype relations. Although, for convenience, geneticists usually use a "constant genotype fitness" model, this has led to a number of paradoxes that can be resolved properly only when phenotypic relations are taken fully into account. (Lewontin 1974, p. 15)

While population genetics has a great deal to say about changes or stability of the frequencies of genes in populations and about the rate of divergence of gene frequencies in populations partly or wholly isolated from each other, it has contributed little to our understanding of speciation and nothing to our understanding of extinction. Yet speciation and extinction are as much aspects of evolution as is the phyletic evolution which is the subject of evolutionary genetics, strictly speaking. (Lewontin 1974, p. 12)

The upshot of all this is that evolutionary theory is, as Morton Beckner[2] insightfully claimed several decades ago (Beckner 1959, pp. 159–172), a family of related models and not an integrated theory such as Newtonian mechanics (see also Sober 1984b, pp. 36–38):

The scientific interest of modern evolutionary theory derives from its success in integrating into a single body of theory the results and data from the most diverse branches of biology: paleontology, genetics, ethology, systematics, biogeography, ecology, etc. (Beckner 1959, p. 159)

My own view is that evolutionary theory consists of a family of related models. . . . Selection theory [by which Beckner means evolutionary theory[3]] is a family of related models that explain or quasi-explain empirical generalizations and particular facts of evolution. The way in which selection theory effects a unification is to be sought in the relations between the models that are applied over the whole range of questions that the fact of evolution raises. (Beckner 1959, pp. 160 and 161)

This fact has important implications for understanding the logical structure of the theory of evolution. These implications are explored in chapter 5. There I maintain that attempts to formalize the theory within a syntactic conception of theory structure have failed. The main reason for this failure, I argue, is that the syntactic conception is illsuited to formalizing theories when the structure of the theory consists of interacting theoretical frameworks. The semantic conception, on the other hand, is well suited to such a task.

1.2. Sociobiology and Testability

In 1975 E.O. Wilson's ground-breaking book *Sociobiology: The New Synthesis* (Wilson 1975) was published. Although a considerable amount of literature that today is considered to be sociobiological existed prior to the publication of Wilson's book, it coalesced prior material into a unified whole and provided it with a disciplinary focus. During the last decade there has been a storm of controversy over the sociobiological enterprise that was formulated in Wilson's book (see, for example, Allen 1976; Caplan 1978; Gould 1976, 1978; Lewontin 1977; Montagu 1980; Sahlins 1976).

In essence, sociobiology is the application of evolutionary theory to the explanation of social behavior where social behavior is broadly understood to include nonintentional behavior such as that of insects like hymenoptera. Consequently, the sociobiological definition of *social behavior* should be carefully distinguished from the vernacular understanding of the term, according to which *social* implies the intentional behavior of individuals engaged in group activity. *Social behavior*, like *altruism* (see Sober in press), is a technical term in sociobiology. Considerable confusion has resulted, and will continue to result, from a failure to distinguish this technical vocabulary from vernacular uses of the same terms.

Sociobiology, therefore, can be characterized as the study of the evolutionary foundations of the interaction (intentional and nonintentional) of individuals within conspecific groups. Sociobiology, for example, investigates, among other things, cooperation and conflict among individuals. Understood in this way, sociobiology involves an extension of the scope of evolutionary theory to social behavior. Hence, if evolutionary theory is a genuine scientific theory, there is a prima facie reason for believing that sociobiology is a genuine scientific enterprise (see Thompson 1980). Whether the extension, as formulated within current sociobiology, of evolutionary theory to social behavior results in a new theory as opposed to a new application of the existing theory of evolution depends on the views of theory structure and theory change that one adopts (for a novel and, I think, insightful analysis of scientific conceptual system change, see Hull 1983, 1985, 1988a, 1988b.) Hence, we shall be in a better position to answer this question after examining conceptions of theory structure.

Despite, however, the prima facie reason just suggested for believing that sociobiology is a genuine scientific enterprise, the actual explanations offered by sociobiologists have made many biologists and philosophers question its scientific status and utility. As indicated in the previous section, a principal assumption of evolutionary theory is that the action of selection on variation in populations results in genetic changes that make the effects of selection heritable. Hence, in order for a characteristic to be the result of evolutionary processes—and therefore amenable to evolutionary explanation—there must be a genetic basis for that characteristic.

This requirement has been seen by a number of critics of sociobiology as its Achilles heel, since the requirement has been widely held to be the basis for one of sociobiology's most serious flaws: its nontestability and therefore its inadequacy as a genuine scientific theory. The most common formulation of this flaw involves pointing out that the attempt by sociobiologists to satisfy the genetic basis requirement results in sociobiological explanations (and, by inference, predictions) that are highly speculative and ad hoc. A central reason for this problem is that the genetic basis of many human behavioral phenomena which are to be explained sociobiologically is unsubstantiated or irrelevant (see Ayala 1987, p. 250). And any evidence that might suggest nongenetic transmission (as, for example, the incredibly short time span—in evolutionary and genetic terms—during which patterns of human social behavior have changed) is rendered impotent by the postulation of ad hoc mechanisms, for example, the multiplier effect. The multiplier effect is, in essence, the principle that the ripple effect of small changes can result in large effects. For example, the removal of ground cover in a small part of an area may set in motion a sequence of effects that result in the entire area becoming a desert.

A mechanism is ad hoc, in a syntactic conception of theory structure, if it cannot be deduced ultimately from the axioms of the theory or more proximately from some laws which can be derived from the axioms. It is ad hoc, in a semantic conception, if it is not part of, or deducible from, the definition of the system. The multiplier effect is therefore ad hoc in both conceptions of theory structure because it is not an axiom of any of the component theories of an evolutionary framework, nor is it deducible from them, and it is not part of the definition of any component system, nor it is deducible from these definitions. It is a mechanism that is introduced to account for a discrepancy between the phenomenon to be explained and the outcome expected on the basis of the theory or theories. This point will become clearer after the discussions of chapters 2 and 4.

These features (the highly speculative and ad hoc character of sociobiological explanations), the critics contend, make the sociobiological enterprise immune to evidence (hence, unscientific) and make sociobiological explanations little more than fascinating storytelling. With slight differences of emphasis, Richard Burian (Burian 1978), Stephen J. Gould (Gould 1976, 1978) and Richard C. Lewontin (Lewontin 1977) have developed this criticism.

In section 6.1 of chapter 6, I argue that although this criticism deals a serious blow to a considerable amount of sociobiological theorizing, it does not strike at the heart of the enterprise. The problem, I argue, can be clearly identified, using a semantic conception of theory structure, as a problem with the application of evolutionary theory to behavioral phenomena (specifically human behavior) and not with the sociobiological enterprise itself. Specifically, it is a problem with the causal sequence of theories employed in relating sociobiological theory to human behavior. This analysis, I contend, is a more thoroughgoing analysis than that provided by the critics and than is possible on a syntactic conception of theories—adherence to which, I argue, has resulted in a failure to correctly diagnose the problem and formulate a solution.

One important outcome of this analysis will be a plausible account of why sociobiological theory is so successfully employed in explaining animal behavior, especially insect behavior—a success freely admitted by some of the critics[4]—and yet so apparently problematic when employed to explain human behavior as well as that of other higher organisms.

In section 6.2, I apply basically the same analysis as in section 6.1 to the more significant question of intelligent human behavior. In section 6.1, I concentrate on behaviors that are the direct result of physiological states such as hormonal changes: for example a fight or flight response. A very large amount of human behavior is, however, not a direct result of physiological states. A great deal of it is mediated by cognitive processes. And the evolutionary explanation of these behaviors, if at all posssible, can be expected to be considerably more complex than physiologically driven behaviors.

I argue in section 6.2 that any account, within an evolutionary framework, of cognitively mediated behavior will involve complex causal chains the links of which are justified by reference to numerous quite distinct theoretical frameworks. The logic of these causal chains can be specified using a semantic conception of theory structure but cannot, in any satisfactory way, be specified using a syntactic conception. Hence, employment of the syntactic conception in formulating the logical structure of explanatory frameworks of cognitively mediated behavior within an evolutionary context will be entirely unsatisfactory. I argue, however, that significant progress can be made by employing a semantic conception of theory structure.

1.3. Culture and the Evolutionary Process

The third foundational issue that I shall examine in light of the discussions of theory structure in chapters 2 and 4 is the role of culture in evolutionary explanations of human behavior and knowledge. In part because of the genetic basis requirement of evolutionary explanation, culture has played no role or, at best, a minimal, and afterthought, role in evolutionary explanations. Attempting, therefore, to place human behavior and knowledge within an evolutionary framework appears to be fundamentally biologically deterministic. Although this attempt poses few problems in the case of evolutionary explanations of insect behavior, knowledge of the world, and learning, it poses enormous problems in the case of evolutionary explanations of human behavior.

There have been a number of attempts by sociobiologists to remedy what they take to be a misunderstanding of their views on this point (see Lumsden and Wilson, 1981, 1983; Dawkins 1982; Ruse 1986; Ruse and Wilson 1986). In general these responses attempt to develop a role for culture within the sociobiological enterprise by emphasizing the capacity of the genetically based structure of the mind to be receptive to culturally transmitted knowledge and patterns of behavior. One result of differential receptivity by different neurobiological structures is differential fitnesses for those structures.

For example, in Dawkins's view, a 'meme' is a unit of information which is "a completely non-genetic kind of replicator, which flourishes only in the environment provided by complex communicating brains" (Dawkins 1982, p. 109). Memes are, in effect, culturally transmitted. For Lumsden and Wilson, genes and culture are "inseverably linked" (Lumsden and Wilson 1983, p. 117), resulting in gene-culture coevolution. In their view, genetically pre-scribed rules of development (epigenetic rules) assemble the mind in ways which allow culture to be absorbed and in which the differential success of the rules in absorbing culture and participating in changing culture in ways that increase fitness will cause the genes, and hence the rule they prescribe, to evolve. Ruse tends to identify with Lumsden's and Wilson's view.

Neither of these attempts to give culture a role, however, are entirely adequate. Memes are culturally transmitted, and insofar as a meme provides a selective advantage to an organism, it provides a selective advantage to the gene which determines the brain structure in which that meme was capable of being encoded. As I hope to indicate in chapter 7, however, this is not a rich enough framework to allow for the kind of complex interaction between genet-ically determined brain structures and cultural information. Cognition is not just environmental and culturally transmitted information stored in a genetically determined brain. Cognition is a complex interaction of neurological structure and environmental and culturally transmitted information. Wilson's and Lums-den's gene-culture coevolution takes even less seriously the extent to which environmental and culturally transmitted information and not just epigenetic rules determine the nature of cognition. What these accounts fail to take seri-ously is the complex interaction of the structural properties of the neurological material with the environmental and culturally transmitted information which results in cognition and cognitive abilities.

What these accounts indicate, however, is that the contexts within which the role of culture in evolutionary explanations of human action and cognition arises with extreme poignancy are the areas of ethics and epistemology. It is in connection with these two aspects of human activity that culture seems extremely important. It is also in these two areas that an evolutionary perspective seems very likely to advance our understanding. This is because it is not unreasonable to expect that ethics and human knowledge are a function, in improtant respects, of our biology; after all, the capacity to formulate codes of right action and conceptions of the nature of the world around us is dependent, in part, on our neurobiology. And since our biology is a product of evolution, the nature of our knowledge can be expected to be influenced by our evolutionary development.

This is the central thesis of Michael Ruse's book, *Taking Darwin Seriously* (1986). According to Ruse, ethics and human knowledge must be explained within an evolutionary framework. Accordingly, he has produced in this book an outline of an evolutionary ethics and of an evolutionary epistemology that is firmly planted within an evolutionary framework. The way, according to Ruse, in which we can take Darwin seriously is by recognizing that we are biological entities that have been shaped by evolution in more ways than physiologically. In addition to physiology, ethics and epistemology have a clear evolutionary determinant. The ways in which we structure our views on right conduct, the ways in which we think, and the strategies we employ to solve problems are the way they are, at least in part, because by being that way they made survival possible.

This application of evolutioary theory to theoretical work on ethics and epistemology is long overdue. However, one must not incautiously believe that just because any complete explanation of ethics and epistemology must take place in an evolutioanry context that evolutionary theory is all that is required to explain ethics and human knowledge. It is not. David Hull has correctly remarked:

> Certain advocates of evolutionary epistemology seem to propose a literal extension of the theory of biological evolution to cover sociocultural phenomena. I happen to think that much more about the behavior traits and social organization of *Homo sapiens* is going to be explicable in strictly biological terms that most of us would like, in particular those traits most closely connected to reproduction. I disagree with those authors who seem to think that such an extension of evolutionary theory is *a priori* impossible. However, I also think that no strictly biological theory is going to explain everything about human sociocultural development, in particular it is not going to explain very much about the changes in the *content* of human conceptual systems. (Hull 1982, p. 274)

In the last chapter of this book, chapter 7, I take Darwin seriously in precisely the way suggested by Ruse: that is, I take seriously the fact that any explanation of ethics and the nature of human knowledge, and any theoretical account of the way in which moral codes and knowledge are acquired, must have an integral evolutionary component. I also take seriously, however, that much more than evolutionary theory is needed to have an adequate theoretical account of ethics and the nature and acquistion of human knowledge. In addition, for example, some account of the mechanisms of cultural information transmission is necessary as well as an account of the ways in which information transmitted culturally affects the acquisition of knowledge.

I argue that, in effect, an adequate theoretical account of human knowledge requires the employment of a number of different theoretical frameworks in an interactive way. Such accounts will consist of complex causal chains, the links of which are grounded by reference to different theories. Consequently, explanations of ethics and epistemology within an evolutionary context will involve complex theoretical frameworks. I argue that the syntactic conception of theories is, and has been, a stumbling block to any formal understanding of the logic of complex theorizing of this kind. And, as with the foundational issues raised in the first two sections of this chapter, I argue that a more useful conception of theories for these cases of complex theorizing is the semantic conception.

Notes

1. The concept of a theory having a lineage which connects past and present theories together such that the identity of a theory is maintained through change over time is quite helpful in understanding theory development. David Hull has developed this idea in numerous publications in recent years (see, for example, Hull 1983, 1985, 1988a, 1988b).

2. Hull (1973) appears to hold a view of evolutionary theory similar to that of Beckner but also seems to hold that evolutionary theory fits the syntactic conception of theory structure and, in arguing for this position, portrays evolutionary theory as a unified theory. For a discussion of this tension in Hull's view, see Thompson in press.

3. My use of the term *selection theory* differs from Beckner's. I use it to designate that theory which describes mechanisms of selection, with the mechanisms of genetics, embryology, and so forth being assumed but not part of the theory. This use is consistent with Rosenberg's use of the term and, I think, with Sober's. Beckner, on the other hand, uses the term as a synonym for *evolutionary theory*: "When I speak of evolutionary theory, I mean that contemporary body of theory that goes by the name of neo-Darwinism, neo-Mendelism, the "synthetic theory," or simply "selection theory"—the term I shall use subsequently (Beckner 1959, p. 160).

4. Consider, for example, Gould's claim (Gould 1976):

Most of *Sociobiology* wins from me the same high praise almost universally accorded to it. For a lucid account of evolutionary principles and an indefatigably thorough discussion of social behavior among all groups of animals, *Sociobiology* will be the primary document for years to come. But Wilson's last chapter, "From Sociobiology to Sociology," leaves me very unhappy indeed. After twenty-six chapter of careful documentation for the nonhuman animals, Wilson concludes with an extended speculation on the genetic basis of supposedly universal patterns of human behavior. (p. 344)

CHAPTER 2

The Syntactic Conception of Theory Structure

In this chapter I outline the main features of a conception of the structure of scientific theories that has exerted the greatest influence on discussions of theory structure in biology. This conception, dubbed by Hilary Putnam as the "Received View" (Putnam 1962),[1] has its roots in logical positivism and held almost universal sway in the philosophy of science from the 1920s until the 1950s. It was worked out primarily in the context of physics, though it was extremely influential in psychology—especially with an operationalist version of the role of correspondence rules (see Bergmann 1951; Bergmann and Spence 1941; Peters 1959; Skinner 1945; Stevens 1935a, 1935b: on operationism see Wilson 1968a, 1968b).

Its main advocate in biology during this period was J. H. Woodger (see Woodger, 1929, 1937, 1939, 1952), who vigorously championed the axiomatic method in biology. In general, however, the conception had only minimal impact in biology and philosophy on discussions of the nature of biology until the 1950s, in large part because very little attention was paid by philosophers of science to the foundations of biology. The first serious philosophical work that examined the foundations of biology was *The Biological Way of Thought* by Morton Beckner (Beckner 1959). Beckner primarily argued for a view of biology which characterized the various kinds of explanation in biology as Humean in structure. This view of explanation was given its most explicit and rigorous formulation by Hempel and Oppenheim in 1948 (Hempel and Oppenheim 1948). During the two decades after the Hempel-Oppenheim formulation, this view was subjected to a wide variety of criticisms (see, for example, Bromberger 1966; Dray 1957; Gallie 1955; Scriven 1958, 1959a, 1959b, 1961, 1962; Taylor 1964). Hempel offered a spirited defense of his formulation (with some significant concessions to his critics) in *Aspects of Scientific Explanation* (Hempel 1965). Beckner, however, did not entirely endorse the logical empiricist conception of science within which this Humean pattern of explanation played a key role and to which the dominant conception of scientific theories set out in this chapter was central.

In my view, Beckner's book constitutes a watershed in the philosophical discussion of the foundations of biology. From that point onward philosophi-

23

cal discussions of biology were more analytic—examining the logical, epistemological, and metaphysical aspects of biology as a science. Hence, the philosophical discussion of biology paralleled the general character of philosophical discussions of physics. Two questions of immediate interest that arose from this parallel general approach were: Is biology a different kind of science than physics? and the corollary, Does biology conform to a logical empiricists conception of science?

Beckner took the position that in many respects biology was like physics and in those respects it did conform to the logical empiricist account of science. In other respects, however, he held it to be different from physics (with regard to functional analysis and the structure of evolutionary theory, for example). In contrast to this position, Thomas Goudge (Goudge 1961) maintained that biology was in most respects different from physics and that, whatever usefulness or descriptive accuracy logical empiricism might have in physics, it was quite inappropriate for biology. In particular, he argued that evolutionary theory could not be structured in the way required by the syntactic conception[2] and that evolutionary explanation was in important ways different from the Humean pattern embedded in logical empiricism. He developed two non-Humean patterns of evolutionary explanation, which he called "integrating explanations" (the logic of which he claimed was more akin to solving a crossword puzzle than to deductive arguments involving laws) and "narrative explanations."

One feature of biology that has received considerable attention is funtional analysis and teleology. Many have seen the presence, in biology, of functional and teleological analysis and explanation as the fundamental difference between biology and physics and the central reason why a logical empiricist conception of science is inappropriate for biology. Nagel (1961), Hempel (1965), and many others have attempted to demonstrate that functional analysis and teleology can be accommodated within a logical empiricist conception. On the the side of the nonassimilation of biology into physical science, Francisco Ayala has written two excellent papers (Ayala 1968, 1970) on this aspect of biology and its significance for biology as an autonomous science. He, quite correctly, places the issue firmly within an evolutionary context.

It was not until the late 1960s and early 1970s that philosophers began to assume and to argue that the logical empiricist conception of science, with its syntactic conception of theory structure, was appropriate for biology and that evolutionary theory and evolutionary explanation could, and ideally should, be structured according to it (see, for example, Ruse 1973; Williams 1970, 1973a, 1973b). The answers these philosophers were giving to the above questions were that biology is not a different kind of science and that the logical empiricist conception of science is, and should be, the appropriate one for characterizing the foundations of biology. As indicated in the introduction to this book, Ruse's book, *The Philosophy of Biology*, was of enormous importance in clarifying the issues and demonstrating the utility of formalization in biology. Unlike Woodger, Ruse was not committed to an axiomatize-before-all-else view but instead used the formal features of the logical empiricist conception to cast light on a number of logical and conceptual features of foundational work in biology. And he gave a penetrating analysis of the problems with conceptions of biological theory and explanation that repudiated a formal approach of the kind offered by logical empiricism.

Even while, and before, Ruse was writing, however, the logical empiricist conception of science was under attack from many different directions quite independent of its applicaiton to biology and was undergoing significant decline (see Suppe 1977). Some criticisms of the conception, such as the *Weltanschauungen* criticisms (see, for example, Kuhn 1962, 1970; Toulmin 1953, 1961; Hanson 1958, 1969a, 1969b), although severely attacking certain aspects of logical empiricism, left the syntactic conception of theory structure unchallenged (see Newton-Smith 1981, pp. 151–156, esp. p. 155)· Others, which I discuss below, identified serious problems with the syntactic conception of theory structure.

David Hull's book, *Philosophy of Biological Science*, was also published in the early 1970s. Although Hull also adopted an analytic, formal approach to the examination of a number of aspects of biological science, he, unlike Ruse, was not completely committed to a logical empiricist conception of science. For Hull, there were significant features of biology which made it less amenable to a logical empiricist conception of science than Ruse had made it appear. Specifically, his views on reductionism (the reduction of Mendelian genetics to molecular genetics in particular) were at odds with the standard logical empiricist account such as is found in *The Structure of Science* (Nagel 1961) (see Hull 1972, 1973, 1974, 1976). Ruse (see Ruse 1971, 1973, 1976), by contrast, cast his discussions of reductionism within the account given by Nagel.

These two books had an enormous impact on the next decade of the philosophy of biology as the discipline struggled for a place in the philosophy of science. They provided a received view on biological science which was quite comprehensive and intelligible to the larger community of philosophers of science. And because of this they initiated, within philosophy, the rise of the philosophy of biology as a serious and exciting part of the philosophy of science. They, in effect, demonstrated that the philosophy of biology was a rich domain of philosophizing.

In this chapter I outline some of the features of the syntactic conception of theory structure that have dominated the philosophy of science in this century, and in subsequent chapters I develop them in the context of biology.

Since my purpose in outlining this conception is to provide a picture of those aspects of the syntactic conception that will later be criticized and compared to the alternative conception for which I am arguing, I provide only the level of detail that seems appropriate to the task at hand. Anyone interested in greater detail and precision or in learning about other features of the syntactic conception should consult the works of Hempel and Carnap or consult one the many excellent general accounts of this conception (see Braithwaite 1953; Nagel 1961; Suppe 1977). And, for a spirited recent defence of the logical positivist conception of science (in particular the deductive-nomological model of explanation) from which logical empiricism and the syntactic conception of theories developed, one should read Fred Wilson's recent book, *Explanation, Causation and Deduction* (Wilson 1985).

Those who think they have a clear understanding of the syntactic conception are encouraged, nonetheless, to read this chapter carefully, since a great deal of subsequent argument is dependent on a clear understanding of the characterization of the conception given here. And, as always, the success of criticisms depends on the particular understanding, by the critic, of the position that is being criticized.

2.1 Formal Languages and Formal Systems

At the heart of the syntactic conception of theory structure are the concepts of a formal language and of a formal system. The importance of formal languages and formal systems for the syntactic conception is found in the role of mathematical logic (first-order predicate logic with identity) in this conception. In the syntactic conception, the logical structure of a scientific theory is that of mathematical logic; that is, the language of the theory and the deductive structure of the theory are the language and deductive structure of mathematical logic: a scientific theory consists of an axiomatization in mathematical logic with an empirical interpretation.

In this section I describe, in an elementary way, the features of formal languages and formal systems. I describe these features from the standpoint of logistic systems (see Copi 1967) in which the term *formal* entails that the elements of a language or system can be completely defined without reference to interpretation. The logistic standpoint is appropriate here because mathematical logic, and the use made of it within the syntactic conception, is a logistic formal system. The concept of a formal system outlined here is therefore quite specific and technical (see appendix A to this chapter).

A formal language consists of a set of well-formed formulas which is determined by specifying, by fiat, a set of symbols and a set of rules for the formation of formulas using the symbols. Although there may exist an intended interpretation for the symbols, it must be possible to specify them independently of any recourse to interpretation. The set of symbols consists of primitive symbols and nonprimitive symbols which must ultimately be defined in terms of the primitive symbols: that is, nonprimitive terms can be defined in terms of other nonprimitive terms only if the chain(s) of definition for any nonprimitive begins with primitives. Formulas are well formed within a formal language if they contain only the symbols of the language and satisfy the rules of formation for the language. Such formulas are called "well-formed formulas" or, in abbreviated form, "wffs."

A formal system consists of a formal language and a deductive apparatus. A deductive apparatus either identifies some of the well-formed formulas of the language as axioms (or postulates) or specifies a set of rules of inference, or both. The axioms are key, or basic, formulas. In general the formulas identified as axioms are so identified with an eye on the intended interpretation of the formal system. Their identification within the system, however, must be possible without recourse to interpretation if the system is to be a formal system. A set of rules of inference specify when one formula is an immediate consequence of other formulas: that is, when a formula is derivable or deducible from other formulas.

When the deductive apparatus for a formal system consists of both a specification of axioms and a specification of a set of rules of inference—this is the case with the syntactic conception of theory structure—some formulas of the system may be theorems that are not axioms. Theorems are either axioms or formulas that can be deduced, in accordance with the rules of inference, from the axioms of the system. Not all well-formed formulas of the language need be theorems of the system. And well-formed formulas that are not theorems may nonetheless be deducible, within a system, from other well-formed formulas. In any deduction, from other formulas, of a well-formed formula that is not a theorem, at least one of the formulas from which it is deduced must be a nontheorem.

Two formal systems can have exactly the same theorems without thereby being identical, since they may have different axioms or different rules of inference. However, two formal languages that consist of the same set of wffs are the same formal language.

2.2. Euclidean Geometry as a Formal System

An examination of the history and structure of Euclidean geometry provides a helpful example of a formal system, of an interpreted formal system, and of the differences between them. In essence, Euclidean geometry can be formulated as a formal system and as a geometry of physical space, in which case it is an interpreted formal system whose domain of application is physical space. Euclidean geometry is most often expounded as an interpreted formal system. Indeed, this is historically how it was expounded and understood.

The point of departure from the view that Euclidean geometry was the geometry of space came in this century with the development of the general theory of relativity. According to this theory, space is non-Euclidean. The goundwork for this change in the conception of space came considerably earlier and consisted principally of two developments: first, the discovery that consistent non-Euclidean geometries could be formulated, and second, following from the first, that mathematical systems could be formulated abstractly— that is, that they could be formulated without regard to possible interpretation. Hence, they need not have any empirical content.

The Greeks raised a question about one of the postulates of Euclid's geometry, the postulate commonly referred to as the "parallel postulate." According to Euclid, two straight lines are parallel if and only if they do not meet when infinitely extended in either direction. Given this definition of 'parallel', the parallel postulate states that one and only one line can be drawn parallel to a given line through a point outside that given line. This is not exactly Euclid's postulate but is logically equivalent to it. What caused the Greeks to be uncertain about this postulate was their knowledge that certain lines that do not meet in a finite distance do meet 'at infinity'. These lines were called "asymptotic." The classic example of asymptotic lines is a hyperbola and its axes: the hyperbola and its axes get closer and closer as they are extended but never meet in a finite distance. In light of this knowledge, it was difficult to take Euclid's parallel postulate as self-evident and therefore as a legitimate axiom of his geometry. The efforts of the Greeks were directed towards demonstrating that it could be deduced from the other postulates of Euclid's geometry. This proof would establish it as a theorem even though it was not self-evident, and hence could not be an axiom. The Greeks and other mathematicians during the next twenty or so centuries failed to develop a proof.

The resolution of this problem had to wait until the nineteenth century, when through the work of Lobachevsky, Riemann, and others a clear demonstration was provided that the parallel postulate could not be derived from any of the other postulates. This impossibility demonstration was, in fact, the outcome of an attempt to develop a proof that the parallel postulate could be derived from the other postulates. The demonstration took the form of an indirect proof: assume that the parallel postulate is false; then attempt to show that all the postulates of Euclid other than the parallel postulate yield a contradiction when combined with the negation of the parallel postulate. Deriving a contradiction would establish that the parallel postulate is derivable from the other postulates, since only if it were could the negation of the postulate contradict anything. This argument does, of course, assume that the rest of Euclid's postulates constitute a consistent set—an issue to which I return below.

The surprising and enormously important result of this attempt was that the negation of the parallel postulate when combined with the other postulates of Euclid could not be shown to lead to a contradiction. Indeed, two new geometries emerged. Two emerged because there are two ways in which the parallel postulate can be negated. One is to assume that no line parallel to a given line can be drawn through a point outside that given line. The second is that more than one line parallel to a given line can be drawn through a point outside that given line. The geometry based on the first assumption is called "spherical geometry" or "Riemannian geometry." The geometry based on the second assumption is called "hyperbolic geometry."

The effects of this development were numerous and profound. The one of relevance here is that it became clear that Euclidean geometry was not the only geometry that could be formulated. And, although it was still regarded as the geometry that described physical space, the way had been opened up for considering the systems of geometry and of mathematics in general as formal systems: that is, for considering mathematical systems as abstract without reference to interpretation, and hence truth. Mathematicians could, and it began to be held, should, develop new systems without reference to their application or truth. The task of pure mathematics is to specify formal systems, investigate the deductive relationships of the formulas of the systems to each other, and investigate the properties of the systems such as completeness and consistency. This changed conception of mathematics created a climate within which numerous new systems were developed, a number of which could not be provided with a familiar interpretation.

The distinction between a formal system and an interpretation for a formal system gives rise to several issues. For example, some account of the nature of interpretation needs to be given. What is an interpretation of a formal system? The answer to this question is that an interpreted formal system is a model of the formal system of which it is an interpretation. A model for a formal system is a structure in which all the theorems of the formal system are true.

Some sense of the nature of models of formal systems can be achieved by considering an important question about formal systems—their consistency—and, in particular, by considering this question in the context of non-Euclidean geometries. Although the consistency of an interpreted formal system is no easier to establish than the consistency of a formal system, psychologically the issues seemed unproblematic prior to the distinction between formal and applied systems. For example, as long as Euclidean geometry was understood as a description of space, the issue of consistency was assumed to be determined by the self-evident character of the axioms. If they were all *obviously* true of space then the system must be consistent. The concepts 'obviously true' or 'self-evidently true' are, as was subsequently learned, not a reliable guide to consistency, but prior to the nineteenth century they appeared to be so. Once the issue of the consistency of formal systems was raised, however, it became clear that new methods for determining consistency—purely formal methods—would need to be developed. New, formal methods for establishing consistency would, if they could be established, supersede the method of appealing to the obvious truth of the axioms because establishing that the formal system was consistent (or inconsistent) would establish that the corresponding interpreted formal system(s) was consistent—(or inconsistent).

Establishing that Riemannian geometry was consistent required more than an appeal to the self-evident character of its axioms because, unlike Euclidean geometry, its axioms have no familiar interpretation. Certainly, they had no empirical interpretation. This point, however, provides a clue to a possible method for establishing its consistency, namely, constructing an abstract model in which all the theorems are true. This method can be used to establish the consistency of some formal systems but proved, however, to be inadequate as a method for proving the consistency of Riemannian geometry. However, the method is instructive with respect to the nature of model interpretations.

The essence of one instance of the model construction method of establishing the consistency of Riemannian geometry is to interpret the terms of the geometry as terms about the surface of a *Euclidean* sphere (Hilbert uses the same method to establish the consistency of Euclidean geometry in terms of a model in Cartesian geometry). Consequently, all axioms of Riemannian geometry become axioms about the sufrace of a *Euclidean* sphere. Riemannian axioms and theorems are transformed into Euclidean axioms and theorems. Unfortunately, this method depends for success upon the prior establishment that Euclidean geometry is consistent. The only conclusion one can draw from this "proof" is that if Euclidean geometry is consistent, then so is Riemannian. Hilbert's attempt to establish the consistency of Euclidean geometry (Hilbert 1899) suffers from the same defect. This proof involves interpreting a point as an ordered pair of real numbers and a line as a linear equation. Real number theory, however, has never been proved consistent. Hence Hilbert's proof establishes only that Euclidean geometry is consistent if real number theory is consistent. This, therefore, is ultmately not a satisfactory method of establishing the consistency of Riemannian geometry.

Although not a successful method for establishing the consistency of Riemannian geometry or, for that matter, most of the important formal systems of mathematics, this example of the method does illustrate well the nature of model interpretations of formal systems. To interpret Riemannian geometry as the geometry of the surface of a Euclidean sphere is to make possible the determination of the truth of the theorems of the system. Indeed, *if* space is held to be Euclidean, it makes possible the determination of the *empirical* truth of the theorems—a point of considerable importance in the context of *scientific* theorizing. What this example illustrates is the way in which model interpretations interpret a formal system by providing a meaning structure for the terms of the formal system such that the theorems of systems are true given that meaning structure. A meaning structure is provided by assigning meanings to the symbols of the formal language of the formal system.

It might appear, on the basis of the foregoing, that the truth of the axioms is all that is required for an interpretation of a formal system to be a model of it. This, however, is not the case, since two formal systems may have the same axioms but may differ in some proof-theoretical way that makes formulas derivable in one not derivable in the other. Hence, a model interpretation of a formal system must be such that all the theorems of the system are true in the model. A final point: a formal system, in principle, can be given more than one interpretaiton.

2.3. Mathematical Logic and the Formal Structure of Scientific Theories

The formal system relevant to syntactic accounts of the structure of scientific theories is first-order predicate logic with identity (mathematical logic). In syntactic accounts, a scientific theory is an interpreted formal system, the formal language of which is identical to to the formal language of the first-order predicate logic with identity. The deductive apparatus consists of the axioms of the specific scientific theory and the rules of inference of first-order predicate logic.[3] As with all formal languages and systems and their interpretations, metatheoretical investigations of scientific theories can be undertaken. For example, as with Euclidean and Riemannian geometry, the completeness and consistency of the axioms of a scientific theory can be investigated.

To understand fully why this conception of theories is referred to as "syntactic" requires a clear understanding of the difference between it and the alternative semantic conception. It is for this reason that I have in my previous writings on this subject preferred to follow Putnam, Suppe, and others and to call it "the received view." This designation, however, is, in my opinion, too pejorative. Moreover, it incorrectly conveys the impression that the logical empiricist view is a monolithic view. It does identify clearly, however, the conception to which I am objecting. I have sometimes referred to this conception as the "statement view of theories" because the theorems of the formal system, under the intended interpretation of the system, are statements (laws) which describes the behavior of phenomena. This designation has the virtue of highlighting one of the key differences between it and the semantic conception, according to which a theory is an extralinguistic entity and not a deductively related set of statements.

On the whole I prefer the designation *syntactic*, since it is the most appropriate contrast to the designation *semantic* for the alternative conception. Moreover, it correctly conveys the very different emphasis of the two conceptions. In the syntactic conception a scientific theory is an interpreted *formal system*. It has, therefore, a syntax given by the formal language and an axiomatic-deductive structure. In a semantic conception a theory is a *model-theoretic structure*. The nautre and significance of this difference in emphasis is the subject of this book and hence, I trust, will be made clearer in subsequent chapters.

In a syntactic conception of theory structure a scientific theory is an axiomatic-deductive system which is partially interpreted in terms of correspondence rules. In this section, I flesh out the first part of this definition, its axiomatic-deductive character; in the next section I discuss correspondence rules and partial interpretation.

According to the syntactic conception of theory structure a theory is formalized in mathematical logic. That means that the formal language of mathematical logic and its rules of inference constitute the formal language of scientific theories and their rules of inference. Some formulas of the formal language are designated as axioms. The designation is made with a clear sense of the intended interpretation of the resultant formal system. At this point, the logical structure of the theory has been determined but no scientific theory has been specified: that is, the syntax of the theory has been given but no semantics has been given. Without an interpretation (a semantics) the theory is abstract and formal without empirical meaning. It is simply a set of deductively related formulas. When interpreted this system consists in a deductively related set of generalizaitons which describe the behavior of phenomena. The generalizaitons form a deductive hierarchy from higher to lower levels of generality. The axioms are generalizations of the highest level of generality (see diagram on the next page).

The most common example of a theory presumed to have this type of deductive structure is Newtonian mechanics. The axioms when interpreted are the three laws of motion and the law of gravitational attraction:

1. Every body tends to remain at rest or in uniform motion unless acted upon by an external unbalanced force;

2. Force equals mass times acceleration ($F = ma$);

3. For every action there is an equal and opposite reaction;

4. The gravitational force of attraction between two bodies is equal to the gravitational constant ($G = 6.66 \times 10^{-s}$ dyne $cm.^2/gm.^2$) times the product of their masses (m_1m_2) divided by the square of the distance betwen them (d^2),

$$F_g = G\ (m_1m_2/d^2).$$

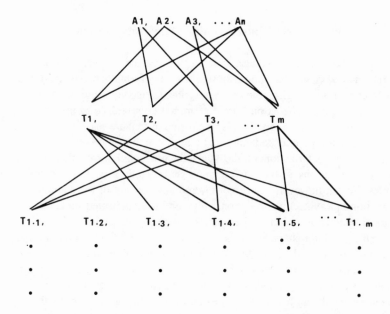

Lines indicate deductive connections. More than one line to a node indicates that the deduction of that theorem requries, as premises, all the theorems for which the lines come. The lines in this diagram illustrate a possible structure.

From these axioms it should be possible, in principle, to deduce all the other laws (interpreted theorems of the formal system) of Newtonian mechanics. It should be possible, in principle, for example, to deduce Galileo's law of free fall ($d = gt^2/2$) Kepler's laws of planetary motion. In practice, numerous simplifying and subsidiary assumptions which are not laws of the theory, but are interpreted wffs of the formal language, are needed in the deduction of these laws. An example of the deduction of Galileo's law from the law of gravitation is given in appendix B to this chapter.

In this view, then, the formal system of a theory is a set of deductively organized formulas whose language and deductive structure are those of mathematical logic. When this formal system is given an empirical interpretation, the resultant structure is a deductively organized set of sentences. Consequently, theories are linguistic structures.

2.4 Empirical Interpretation of a Formal System

Up to this point, I have characterized the syntactic aspects of scientific theories in a syntactic conception. In summary, the formal language and rules of inference for scientific theories in syntactic accounts are supplied by mathematical logic. The axioms are determined by reference to the intended domain of the specific theory: that is, the formulas that are selected as axioms are selected with the intended empirical interpretation of the system in mind. During the characterization of the syntactic aspects, I have alluded on a number of occasions to the interpretation or semantic aspects of scientific theories. So far, however, I have not offered any account of the nature of interpretation in a syntactic conception, although I have indicated some features of model interpretation in the discussion of geometry in section 2.2.

In this section I characterize the specific nature of interpretation in a syntactic conception of the structure of scientific theories. At the outset, I emphasize that this is an extremely important part of the syntactic conception. Without a satisfactory method of interpreting the formal system part of a scientific theory, the theory has no adequate empirical meaning. A scientific theory, in the syntactic view, therefore, consists of *both* a formal system and an interpretation. Both are essential components.

As was indicated in section 2.2, constructing a model interpretation for a formal system involves specifying a meaning for the symbols of the formal language. This is done for scientific theories by employing correspondence rules. These rules, along with an interpretation of some of the symbols as referring to directly observable entities and their properties, provide a model for the formal system in which all the theorems of the system are empirically true. The model is the phenomenal world. The relevant nonlogical symbols (i.e., constants) of a theory are of two kinds: 1) symbols that are interpreted as referring directly to observable physical entities or their properties (these are part of the observation vocabulary of the theory); 2) symbols that are interpreted as referring to entities or their behavior which cannot be directly observed (these are part of the theoretical vocabulary of the theory).

Correspondence rules provide an empirical interpretation of the symbols in the theoretical vocabulary by partially defining them in terms of the observation vocabulary. This method of partial definition assumes that a distinction between observation terms and theoretical terms can be made.[4] Consequently, correspondence rules provide a link between the observation language (phenomenal world) and the theoretical language (theoretical world). The logical structure of correspondence rules and their role in theories underwent considerable development from the early 1920s to the 1950s (see Suppe 1977 for an excellent account of the historical development of the syntactic conception—which he refers to, following Putnam, as "the received view"—and of correspondence rules within it). Originally correspondence rules were understood to provide explicit definitions of theoretical terms. In response to numerous difficulties with this understanding, they were subsequently understood to provide partial definitions of the theoretical terms. In the later and most sophisticated formulations of Hempel (see Hempel 1965, especially "Empiricist Criteria of Cognitive Significance: Problems and Changes" and "The Theoretician's Dilemma: A Study in the Logic of Theory Construction") and Carnap, partial interpretation is provided by correspondence rules in the form of bilateral reduction sentences. In this conception, correspondence rules have the general form

$$Cx \rightarrow (Qx \leftrightarrow Ex),$$

where C is an observation term describing a test condition, Q is a theoritcal term, and E is an observation term describing an outcome under the test condition (see Hempel 1965, pp. 188–189). Hence, a theoretical term like *fragile* will be partially defined

$$(x)(t)(Sxt \rightarrow (Fx \leftrightarrow Bxt).$$

In other words, for any thing 'x' and for any time 't' if 'x' is struck sharply at 't' then 'x' is fragile if and only if 'x' breaks at 't' (see Hempel 1965, pp. 109–110).[5]

Two important features of the syntactic conception of theory structure can now be emphasized. First, correspondence rules are an integral part of the theory. Without the correspondence rules, only a formal system remains. It is correspondence rules that make it a *scientific* theory and not just a formal system without empirical meaning.[6] Second, correspondence rules specify the ways in which the theory is applied to phenomena. Since the meaning of the nonobservational, nonlogical terms of a theory is provided by correspondence rules which relate these theoretical terms to observational terms, the ways in which entities and properties of entities denoted by theoretical terms affect entities denoted by observational terms are determined by the correspondence rules.

Take the example of *fragile* given above. To claim that something is fragile relative to a particular theory is to claim that the entity, under certain observable conditions, will break. The conditions are spelled out by the correspondence rules. Hence, a theory that contains the term *fragile* and has the above correspondence rule will specify by means of that correspondence rule how the theory is to be applied to a Waterford crystal sherry glass. To claim that according to the theory that the sherry glass is fragile is to claim that under conditions specified by the correspondence rule the glass will break.

These two features of the syntactic view entail that it is not possible to distinguish between a theory and the ways in which it is applied to the world. The theory contains, in its correspondence rules, the specifications for the ways in which it applies to the world. And without correspondence rules there is no scientific theory. The upshot of this is that the correspondence rules determine a model of the formal system part of a theory such that the model is taken to be identical with the empirical phenomena within the scope of the theory. The theory is therefore taken to be a linguistic description of the causal behavior and structure of empirical phenomena.

2.5. Laws, Explanation, Prediction, and Testing

In this conception, laws are interpreted theorems of the formal system with the axioms of the system becoming, under interpretation, the axioms of the theory (which are themselves laws). As a consequence of the hierarchical structure of the theorems of formal systems whose language and deductive rules are those of mathematical logic, the laws of a scientific theory are hierarchically organized. At the highest level of the hierarchy are the axioms. At the lowest level are laws all of whose terms are observational terms. The axioms of the theory are laws of the highest generality which cannot be deduced from any other set of laws, including any set of the remaining axioms. All other laws, can, in principle, be deduced from the axioms. In practice numerous subsidiary assumptions need to be added to the laws in order to allow anything approaching a deduction of laws from laws.

A scientific theory, in this conception, is therefore a partially interpreted set of laws which are organized in an axiomatic-deductive structure. These laws describe the behavior of phenomena and allow the explanation and prediction (by means of which they are testable) of the behavior of particular phenomena. Ideally, explanation is achieved by citing some prior conditions of the system and by citing laws that describe the causal connection between these conditions and the event to be explained. This conception of explanation, variously called "deductive-nomological," "covering law," and "subsumption under general laws," has the general pattern

$$\frac{L_1, L_2, \ldots, L_n}{C_1, C_2, \ldots, C_m}$$
$$E$$

Where L_1–L_n are relevant laws, C_1–C_m *are relevant initial conditions, and E* is the event to be explained.

The logical relationship of the laws and prior conditions to the event being explained is ideally deductive, but when, as is often the case, some of the laws are statistical, it is inductive. This pattern has the logical form of Modus Ponens, in which the laws are statements of the form

$$(x)(Px \, -> \, Qx).$$

Prediction in this conception has the same logical structure as explanation but has different temporal parameters. In their original formulation Hempel and Oppenheim (Hempel and Oppenheim 1948) considered explanation and prediction to be symmetrical; that is, any explanation prior to the occurrence of the event being explained would have been a prediction, and any prediction whose initial conditions are fulfilled becomes an explanation of the event that was previously predicted. Numerous counterexamples to this symmetry can be given. Most demonstrate that many legitimate predictions fail to be acceptable explanations after the event has occurred. For example, one can predict the height of a flagpole by deducing the height from the length of the shadow it casts combined with the angle between the sun and the horizon and the laws of geometric optics (see Bromberger 1966). The same deductive pattern, though conforming to the Hempel-Oppenheim pattern, is not considered by most to be an acceptable explanation because no causal connection is described by the laws of geometric optics. A notable exception is Bas van Fraassen who, taking an Aristotelian teleogical perspective, has quite persuasively argued that the length of a flagpole's shadow can explain its height (see van Fraassen 1980, pp. 130–134). Other counterexamples to the symmetry involve the use of symptoms or signs to predict a future event. Three widely discussed examples are the use of Koplik spots to predict a measles rash; syphilis to predict, in untreated persons, paresis; and changes in the reading on a barometer to predict changes in the weather. Despite these counterexamples, what remains the case is the commitment on the part of logical empiricists to the sameness of the logical structure of explanation and causal prediction.

A law is confirmed by testing the causal connections it asserts—that is, by experimentally bringing about, or identifying the natural occurrence of, its antecedent conditions and ascertaining whether its consequent follows. Testing a large number of the laws of a theory or a part of a theory increases the probability of the truth of the theory. Since the laws of a theory are deductively interrelated, confirmation of any law indirectly supports all the other laws. The pattern for these tests is

$$T \rightarrow (C \rightarrow R).$$

In other words, if the theory is true, then if test condition C is true (occurs), result R is true. $(C \rightarrow R)$ is in effect a law of the theory. T can also be a hypothesis about the behavior of a restricted set of phenomena from which certain generalizations about the causal connections between events can be inferred. Confirmation of hypotheses is logically the same as confirmation of theories or parts of theories.

The pattern set out above is inductive. The occurrence of R given the occurrence of the test conditions C does not deductively entail that T is true. To argue thus would be to commit the fallacy of affirming the consequent. However, assuming that the number of generalizations to be tested for any theory is finite, each successful test reduces by one the number of remaining possible tests, and hence reduces by one the probability that the theory will be disconfirmed. In effect, each successful test decreases the probability that the theory is false, and thereby increases the probability that it is true.

Although Karl Popper generally accepts the syntactic conception, he rejects this feature. He rejects induction and denies that confirmation of theories is possible. Instead he argues for a methodology based on falsification rather than verification and confirmation. Simply put, his view is that it is the job of science to put forward bold theories and hypotheses and then seek to falsify them, thereby weeding out the false but never asserting truth or even probable truth of any individual theory or hypothesis (see Popper 1959, 1965). Of course, abandoning truth in this way has important consequences in connection with the notions of the rationality of science and the growth of scientific knowledge. In order not to abandon the rationality of science and measures of the growth of scientific knowledge, Popper employs the concept 'verisimilitude' in place of 'truth' (see Newton-Smith 1981, pp. 44–76, for an excellent account of this feature of Popper's philosophy of science and of the problems with it).

As can be seen, there are numerous attractive features to this conception of theory structure. It provides an integrated account of the logical structure of theories, how theoretical terms acquire empirical meaning, how events are explained and predicted, how laws and theories are tested, and how hypotheses which are based on a theory are tested. In addition, as with axiomatization in other contexts (including definitions of axiomatic theories by set-theoretical predicates, as in Suppes' (1957, 1967) set-theoretical semantic conception of scientific theories), this account of the formal structure of theories makes possible the importation of important formal results form other domains of theorizing. This results from the fact that first-order predicate logic is a common demoninator in all scientific theories and in many other theories. Hence, with modification to fit this context, the following claim by Stoll encapsulates this point:

> A by-product of the creation of an axiomatic theory which is the common denominator of several theories is the possibility of enriching and extending given theories in an inexpensive way. For example, a theorem in one theory may be the origin of a theorem in the derived theory and, in turn, may yield a new result in another parent theory. In addition to the possible enrichment in content of one theory by another, by way of an axiomatic theory derived from both, there is also the possibility of "cross-fertilizaiton" insofar as methods of attack on problems are concerned. That is, a method of proof which is standard for one theory may provide a new method in another theory with a derived theory serving as a linkage. (Stoll 1963, pp. 226–227)

2.6. Criticisms of This Conception

Both the syntactical and semantic components of this conception have been severely criticized. In this section I describe only those criticisms which are relevant to later discussions. This means that a large number of the criticisms that have been made in the literature—many of which I endorse—will not be discussed here. For example, I do not discuss Putnam's (Putnam 1962) and Achinstein's (Achinstein 1963, 1968) criticisms that the observation-theoretical distinction, which is fundamental to the syntactic conception, cannot be made. On this point see the argument of Suppe (Suppe 1972a), who for different reasons rejects the syntactic view but argues that the observation-theoretic distinction can be adequately made. Neither do I discuss the important attack by Quine on the analytic-synthetic distinction assumed by the syntactic conception. Nonetheless, the criticisms that are discussed below are more than adequate to justify a rejection of the syntactic conception.

Patrick Suppes (Suppes 1968) has pointed out that scientific theories which are axiomatized in first-order predicate logic with identity are, in fact, only quasiaxiomatizations: that is, they assume set theory, number theory, and other mathematical theories. The axioms of these other theories are not among the axioms of the scientific theory. Hence, the axiomatization is not a strict axiomatization: it relies on formulas and interpretations of those formulas which are not among its theorems, although they are among the theorems of other formal systems. Consequently, scientific theories are what Robert Stoll has called "informal theories" (Stoll 1961, pp. 227–232): that is, they are axiomatic theories that presuppose, as already known, other theories (such as general set theory).

This, in itself, is not a very serious criticism of the syntactic conception, since numerous mathematical theories are also infomal theories. For example, group theory and natural number theory as axiomatized using Peano's axioms (see Stoll 1961, pp. 228–230) are informal theories—both presuppose as already known a theory of inference and general set theory. What it does indicate, however, is the complexity of axiomatic theories and the elaborate nature of these structures. This complexity should at least cast doubt on the possibility of achieving axiomatizations in first-order predicate logic of most scientific theories. There is, however, an even more significant consequence of the recognition that, as axiomatic theories, scientific theories are informal theories.

Since scientific theories are informal theories which presuppose general set theory, one can take advantage of the power of general set theory to express the scientific theory by defining the theory by means of a set-theoretical predicate. This fact is the basis of Suppes' set-theoretical approach to the formalization of scientific theories. The details of this approach are given in chapter 4, section 4.5. Suffice it to say here that the criticism of the syntactic conception that arises from the recognition that, in this conception, scientific theories are informal theories is that axiomatization in mathematical logic is extremely complex and not the most mathematically powerful or formally useful way to formalize a scientific theory.

On an entirely different front, Kenneth Schaffner (1968) and Patrick Suppes (1962) have criticized the role of correspondence rules in the syntactic conception. Though identifying different problems, the common feature of their criticisms is that the ways in which theories relate to the world are complex and inadequately represented by the correspondence rules of the syntactic conception.

First, the syntactic conception misleadingly entails that any changes in the procedures for applying the theory will result in a new theory and not, as seems a more felicitous description, in new ways of applying the same old theory.

Second, specifying the procedures for applying the theory to phenomena by means of correspondence rules which are part of the theory does not provide an accurate representation of the kinds of ways in which theories are applied to phenomena. Kenneth Schaffner has convincingly argued that specifying the ways in which a theory relates to phenomena in terms of correspondence rules ignores the ways in which laws from other independent theories are employed in "causal sequences" which causally related theories to phenomena. These causal sequences describe the causal mechanisms underlying the measurement and observation procedures which are used to apply the theory: that is, they explain why the measuring device or observation apparatus behaves the way it does, and hence why it is acceptable to use a particular procedure to obtain observations relevant to the theory. Since the correspondence rules of the syntactic conception provide no role for laws of other theories in the relating of a particular theory to phenomena, two distinct theories cannot be interactively employed (see Nagel et al. 1962).

For example, the theoretical term *chromosome* in a theory about chromosomal segregation during meiosis is connected to observation terms by correspondence rules which will link the term to entities which have certain physical characterisitcs, staining properties, locations in a cell, behaviors, and so forth, as seen using a light microscope or an electron microscope. In order to explain, however, just why what is seen using the microscope should have anything to do with chromosomes, one needs to provide a causal account of how the microscope works: that is, in order to assert the connection asserted by the correspondence rules, one needs to employ laws of optics (in the case of a light microscope) or laws of subatomic physics (in the case of an electron microscope). Therefore, relating theories to the world involves employing the laws and correspondence rules of other theories in causal sequences which render comprehensible the rationale for providing the link. And the correspondence rules of the borrowed theories, when used to provide a causal sequence linking a designated theory with phenomena, are different in kind from the correspondence rules of the designated theory.[7]

In the syntactic conception these other laws and correspondence rules play no role in relating the theory to the world. Hence, it does not provide an accurate account of the ways in which several theories can be used to provide a causal sequence in which borrowed theories link a designated theory with observation reports.

Third, the syntactic conception provides a distorted picture of the experimental procedures employed in relating theories to phenomena. As Suppes has argued, there is a hierarchy of theories which mediate between a designated theory and an experimental situation.

Suppes has identified three theories which, along with numerous unstated ceteris paribus conditions, mediate between a physical theory (which stands at the top of the hierarchy of theories) and phenomena: the theory of the experiment, the theory of data, and the theory of experimental design (which is where the ceteris paribus conditions are relevant). Possible realizations of the theories are models of the theories.

The theory of experimental design is employed to structure an experiment. The randomization of the assignment of subjects to groups, the materials to be used, the methods of administering drugs or tests, the relationship of the output of instruments to the characteristics and behavior of phenomena, and so forth are part of the theory of experimental design. In structuring the experiment, the theory of experimental design will frequently employ other theories in causal sequences of the kind outlined by Schaffner. For example, relating the behavior of chromosomes to observed images produced by a light microscope under certain experimental conditions will require the employment of a theory of optics as well as a theory about staining tissues, and so forth. Part of what the theory of experimental design does is to specify some of the causal sequences which Schaffner has identified as being involved in relating theories to phenomena. In addition to the stated structure produced by the theory of experimental design, numerous unstated ceteris paribus conditions (for example, noise levels, the amount of sleep a subject had the previous night, background electromagnetic radiation) will be taken into account at the level of implementing the conditions described by a realization of the theory of experimental design.

The theory of data is employed to relate the relevant entities and their behavior in a phenomenal system to the relevant parameters of the particular physical system which is claimed to be isomorphic to the phenomenal system. In other words, a realization of the theory of data will identify entities and their behavior at the phenomenal level with the parameters of a particular physical system and will describe conditions of adequacy of fit (usually statistical tests) between the phenomena and the parameters of the physical system. As with theories of experimental design, theories of data will often employ other theories in causal sequences of the kind described by Schaffner.

A realization of the theory of data allows a comparison of the results of the experiment, which are in terms of observed entities and their behavior, with the predictions of the physical system described by the theory of the experiment. This comparison is usually carried out in terms of statistical tests of goodness of fit.

The theory of the experiment appears, for Suppes, to be employed to select from all the possible physical systems described by the theory those which, if the theory is true, represent the particular experimental framework under investigation. In other word, it is used to induce a class of causally possible physical systems which represent the experimental framework (see Suppes 1967).

In these three ways correspondence rules fail to accurately capture the complexity and richness of the relationship between a theory and phenomena (see also van Fraassen 1981). One major problem with correspondence rules is that they are part of the theory and they specify the ways in which the theory relates to the world.

Another problem with the syntactic view it that two or more theories cannot easily or naturally be employed interactively in order to provide a coherent account of phenomena. The theories which are to be interactivley employed must be simultaneously axiomatized in a single theory in order to make possible a conjoint employment of them. This is seldom possible or desirable because such simultaneous axiomatization will be complex and unmanageable. This problem is at the heart of the difficulties involved in providing an axiomatization in first-order predicate logic of evolutionary theory (see chapter 4). The primary reason that the conjoint employment of several theories requires a simultaneous axiomatization in a single theory of the component theories is that correspondence rules provide a global meaning structure for the axiomatized formal system of the theory. Since different theories will have different global meaning structures, they cannot interact. Some terms of one theory will not occur in the other theory or theories. Hence, they will be meaningless in the other theory, or whatever meaning they are given will be different from the meaning given in the first theory because they will be given meaning with a *different global* meaning structure. And, since the global meaning structure constitutes a model of the formal system such that the theorems of the formal system are *laws of nature*, different theories will be describing, through their laws of nature, different phenomenal systems (natures). These descriptions may or may not be consistent.

In chapters 3, 5, 6, and 7 I indicate how these features of the syntactic account negatively affect the understanding, and discussion, of foundational issues in evolutioanry biology.

2.7. Summary

The conception of theories which still dominates the philosophy of science is a conception that has its roots in logical positivism (see Suppe 1977 for an excellent exposition and historical account of this conception; see also Braithwaite 1953; Carnap 1936, 1937; Hempel 1965, 1967). It is this conception that underlies the accounts of evolutionary theory given by a number of philosophers of biology (see, for example, Ruse 1973; Hull 1974; Rosenberg 1985). It is also the account that many biologists, if pressed, will produce as the correct logical structure of evolutionary theory.

In this conception, dubbed by one of its critics—Hilary Putnam (Putnam 1962)—"the received view," a scientific theory is an axiomatic deductive structure which is partially interpreted in terms of definitions called "correspondence rules." Correspondence rules define the theoretical terms of the theory by reference to observation terms.

For example, a theoretical term like *voltage* is partially defined by reference to readings on a calibrated meter such as a galvanometer. The definition is only partial because a term can be defined by reference to an open-ended number of observational situations and procedures. New technologies, for example, will make possible new observations and new empirical operations, and if the term were explicitly rather than only partially defined by a particular operation, the new technological procedure would, in effect, amount to a re-definition rather than simply an expansion of the definition of the term.

For some theoretical terms empirical meaning is indirect: that is, some theoretical terms are defined by reference to one or more other theoretical terms. Ultimately, any chain of such definitions must end in theoretical terms that are defined by reference to observations. Because of this complex inter-connection of theoretical terms, the meaning of any one term is seldom inde-pendent of the meaning of many if not all of the other terms of the theory. Hence, theories have a global meaning structure: changes to the meaning of one term will have consequences for the meaning of many and usually all the other terms of the theory.

Hence, in the syntactic conception, a theory consists of a set of deduc-tively related statements, the structure of which is provided by mathematical logic and the empirical meaning of which is provided by definitions in terms of correspondence rules which link theoritical terms like *mass, electron, spin, gene,* and so forth to other theoretical terms or to observations. Ultimately these definitions provide direct or indirect partial empirical meaning to all the terms of the theory. In this way the theory as a whole is given empirical mean-ing.

The statements of which a theory consists are generalizations (laws), a small subset of which are taken as the axioms of the theory. The axioms are laws of the highest generality within the theory. They constitute a consistent set, no one of which can be derived from any subset of the others. All laws of a theory, including the axioms, describe the behavior of phenomena. All laws except the axioms, in principle, can be derived from the axioms. Usually such deductions require numerous subsidiary assumptions. The explanation and prediction of phenomena consist in demonstrating that the phenomena can be deduced (or that they follow logically with a high probability) from some subset of the laws of the theory conjoined with a relevant description of the prior state of the system.

The features of this conception that are relevant to the thesis of this book are as follows: (1)   the logical structure of scientific theories is that of a for-mal system whose language and rules of inference are those of mathematical logic; (2) the definitions, in terms of correspondence rules, which provide meaning to (that is, semantics for) the formal system are an essential part of the theory, without which the deductive structure would be empirically mean-ingless; (3) the definitions provide the link between theory and phenomena by virtue of their defining the terms of the theory by reference to phenomenal observations; (4) because of (3) the theory specifies the way in which it relates to the world.

Appendix A

In the philosophic literature there is no common use of the terms *formal language* and *formal system*. Nor is there a common understanding of the relationship between the two. For example, Kyburg claims the following:

> A strict formal system consists of two parts:
>   I. A calculus
>   II. An interpretation (Kyburg 1968, p. 9),

whereas Geoffrey Hunter claims the following:

> The essential thing about a formal language is that, even if it is given an interpretation, *it can be commpletely defined without reference to any interpretation for it:* and it need not be given any interpretation.

> It must be possible to define both sets [symbols and formation rules] without reference to interpretation: otherwise the language is not a formal language.

> By specifying a deductive apparatus for a formal language we get a formal system.

> The deductive apparatus must be definable without reference to any intended interpretation of the language: otherwise the system is not a formal system. (Hunter 1971, pp. 4–7)

The essential difference between Kyburg and Hunter is that Kyburg builds into his definition of a formal system the requirement of an interpretation, whereas Hunter explicitly excludes this requirement, making it a condition of a system being formal that both the language and the deductive apparatus (these together constitute what Kyburg calls a "calculus") be definable without reference to interpretation.

Moreover, as is clear from the above quotations from Hunter, he considers a formal language to be part of a formal system (as apparently does Kyburg). Charles Caton, however, in his entry in *The Encyclopedia of Philosophy*, claims the following:

> Artifical languages in the philosophical sense are also sometimes called *formal*, formalized, symbolic, or ideal languages.

> An artificial language may be characterized more explicitly as an inter-

preted formal system. A formal (or logistic) system in the sense involved here is a symbolism whose structure and manipulation are strictly specified by rules giving the vocabularies and syntax of the system. (Caton 1967, p. 168: emphasis added)

It appears that Caton's formal system is identical to Hunter's formal language, and that an artificial language is a Caton formal system plus interpretation. Hence, an artifical language for Caton is Hunter formal language plus interpretation.

In this book, I am using Hunter's terminology, since mathematical logic—the specific formal system which plays an important role in the syntactic conception of the structure of scientific theories—is a formal system in the sense of a logistic formal system. A logistic formal system is one in which the set of symbols, the set of formation rules, the set of axioms, and/or the set of transformation rules are completely defined without reference to interpretation. This feature of the formal system of mathematical logic is extremely important to understanding the syntactic conception of theory structure and the criticisms of it dealt with in this book.

In addition, as the discussion of geometries as formal systems in section 2.2 indicated, there is a significant value in defining formal systems such that they do not include interpretations. This value bacame clear with the development of non-Euclidean geometries (see Nagel and Newman 1968).

Appendix B

Newton's second law is

$$F = ma.$$

Hence

$$a = F/m.$$

In the context of a free-falling body, F is the force of gravitational attraction (which equals the gravitational mass, m_g, times the gravitational force per unit mass, g), and m_I is the inertial mass. If one makes the simplifying assumption that for objects at low speeds air resistance is negligible,* the resulting equation is

$$a = m_g g / m_I.$$

Since m_g/m_I is constant for all objects and since, by defining m_I and m_g in terms of the same kilogram standard, m_I is made equal to m_g, the ratio m_g/m_I can be disregarded. Consequently, for a free-falling body

$$a = g.$$

Moreover, since g does not change direction or magnitude to any appreciable degree unless the distance moved through becomes comparable to the size of the earth, it is possible to make the additional simplifying assumption that acceleration is constant in all cases where gravity is the sole important force and the acceleration is equal to g. Consequently, since

$$a = v/t,$$

then

$$v/t = g,$$

which is equivalent to

$$v = gt.$$

Integrating velocity with respect to time to get distance,

$$d = \int gtdt,$$

yields

$$d = gt^2/2,$$

which is Galileo's law of free fall.

Notes

1. Putnam's designation accurately suggests the sway that this view held for a

---

*If the force of air resistance (F_a) is not ignored, the resulting equation is

$$a = (F_a + m_g g)/m_I.$$

This derivation is considerably more complicated.

considerable part of this century as does Feigl's reference to it as the "orthodox" view (see Feigl 1970).

2. Thomas Goudge (Goudge 1961) argued that not only could evolutionary theory not be structured according to a received view but that the enterprise was fraught with problems and should not be attempted. Biology, according to Goudge, was a different kind of science from physics and chemistry and required different models of theory structure, explanation, and prediction. Morton Beckner (Beckner 1959) held a more accommodating position. He did not argue that biology was different from physics but that evolutionary theory was not appropriately organized for formalization according to the received view. He considered evolutionary theory to be a family of related models and not a unified structure. Unlike Goudge, however, he did argue for the similarity of some aspects of physics and biology (for example, the logic of Humean explanation).

3. Carnap in 1956 allowed that first-order logic may need to be augmented by modal operators. The motivation for this addition seems to be the inadequacy of reduction sentences in handling dispositional properties and the acceptance that scientific laws and counterfactual conditionals are nonextensional and fundamentally causal. This latter point entails that laws and counterfacutal conditionals can only be specified using a nonextensional logic of causal modalities. Acceptance of this position is due in large measure to articles by Chisholm (Chisholm 1946) and Goodman (Goodman 1947) and the wealth of literature they spawned.

4. Whether this distinction can be made has been the subject of controversy, and critics of the distinction have taken the reliance of the received view on this dubious distinction to be one of its major flaws (see, for example, Putnam 1962). One effect of the works of Hanson (1958), Kuhn (1962), and Feyerabend (1965) was to call the tenability of this distinction into question.

5. James MacAllister has quite correctly pointed out to me in a personal communication that Hempel's exposition (Hempel 1965) does not capture important features of interpretation in this conception and does not accurately reflect the earlier work of Carnap (Carnap 1939, 1936), Feigl (Feigl 1970), and others. He developed these views in a research paper for my philosophy of biology graduate course. Essentially, his argument is that examples like *fragile* do not involve the coordination of a physical magnitude with a theoretical parameter. Hence, in Hempel's example, *break* is as uninterpreted as *fragile*. A genuine observation would be a reading on a calibrated scale, that is, a physical magnitude. For the purposes of this book, however, nothing significant is lost by adhering to Hempel's exposition.

6. One might think that the actual scientific theory could be taken to be just an appropriate formal system: that is, the actual theory could be a formal system whose axioms are appropriate for the scientific purposes to which the system will be put when interpreted. There are several problems with this. First, and most obviously, theories, in this view, have no meaning, and to call them "scientific theories" is at least bizarre. Second, in this view, it is in principle possible for one scientific theory (formal system) to be interpreted differently in different scientific contexts so that what would be two different scientific theories if the interpretation were included is, in this view, only one

scientific theory. Third, appropriate axioms could be chosen only if one already knew what interpretation the system would be given. Hence, a specific set of correspondence rules would be used to determine the formal system. Hence, the theory viewed as a formal system already presupposes specific correspondence rules as part of the theory. Fourth (a problem for realists), if theories are only formal systems, then theories cannot be true or false.

7. Even a formalization that unified two particular theories would be of limited value, since other theories would be required to describe the causal mechanisms underlying the measurement procedures specified by the correspondence rules of the new unified theory—unless, of course, as Ronnie de Sousa pointed out to me, the unification resulted in an all-encompassing ultimate theory. For all actual cases of the formalization of subultimate theories, the above point holds.

CHAPTER 3

Syntactic Conceptions of Evolutionary Theory

As remarked in the last chapter, the syntactic conception of theory structure has been an extremely influential conception for most of the last century. And, in the context of biology, it has been pivotal. Indeed, the extent of its pivotal role can be seen in the fact that in many respects the arguments for the view that biology was a different kind of science than physics or that formalization was of no, or very limited, use in biology were motivated by a desire to establish that biology was a genuine science even though it failed to conform to many of the features of the syntactic conception. In essence, the syntactic conception was perceived to be so entrenched in the understanding of the paradigm science, physics, that those who held that evolutionary theory did not conform to the syntactic conception but was none the less respectable science were forced to argue that biology was logically and methodologically different from physics. The alternative to this position was to argue that biology was not a different kind of science and that it did conform, in essence, to the syntactic conception. The syntactic conception was taken to be an ideal—an ideal that biology fell short of meeting not because it was an inappropriate standard but because it was a very complex and a very young science by comparison with physics. These alternatives, I am suggesting, are false alternatives: biology is not logically or methodologically different from physics, nor does it conform to the syntactic conception of theory structure. The correct alternative is to reject the syntactic conception of theory structure for physics and biology—indeed, for all sciences.

In the previous chapter I set out a number of general criticisms of the syntactic conception. In this chapter I focus on the specific nature of one of these criticisms by examining two influential attempts to provide an account of evolutionary theory in a syntactic conception. In my view, these two attempts are the most explicit and detailed syntactic conception accounts available. They are Michael Ruse's sketch of the axiomatic structure of population genetics, which he argues is the core of evolutionary theory (Ruse 1973) and Mary Williams' axiomatization of the theory of natural selection (Williams 1970; see also Williams 1973a, 1973b). Alexander Rosenberg, alone (see Rosenberg 1985) and in collaboration with Williams (see Rosenberg and Williams 1986), has recently offered a vigorous defence of Williams' axiomatization and the priority of 'fitness', which I examine below.

After explicating these two accounts, I review the criticisms of them that have been offered. These criticisms, I argue, show effectively that syntactic conception accounts are fundamentally flawed. The fundamental flaw is that they cannot represent the fact that evolutionary 'theory', as indicated in chapter 1, is not a unified theory but a theoretical framework composed of a family of interacting theories. Hence, although in some very distant future a unified theory may be formulated, at present syntactic conception accounts are inadequate. An adequate formalization of 'theory' must be capable of representing theory interaction, which syntactic conception accounts cannot do.

I have used scarequotes around the word *theory* in order to indicate a difficulty encountered in using the same expression, *theory*, to refer to two structurally quite different entities. On the one hand, *theory* is taken by Ruse, Williams, and Rosenberg to refer to a deductively and semantically unified description of the causal mechanisms of evolution. On the other hand, in my view of the structure of evolutionary theory, *theory* refers to a complex framework of interacting unified 'theories' which as *a whole* describes the causal mechanisms of evolution. For clarity, I shall, where confusion might otherwise occur, either enclose the term *evolutionary theory* in scarequotes or use the expression *framework* to denote evolutionary 'theory' as I understand it. This approach permits the expression *evolutionary theory* used without scarequotes to retain the meaning it has in the writings of Ruse, Williams, Rosenberg and others: a unified description.[1] I always mean by 'evolutionary theory' or 'an adequate evolutionary theoretical framework' the modern synthetic theory of evolutionary (or neo-Darwinism).

The adoption of this convention should not be taken to indicate that, in my view, 'evolutionary theory' is not really a genuine scientific theory after all but rather a collection of theories. It is a genuine scientific theory even though its structure is that of a complex framework of intereacting theories. I hold that it is a theory because it has all of the functional properties of a theory, and I maintain that the appropriate criteria for determining whether a framework is a theory are functional criteria. Specifically, a theory functions to explain and make intelligible phenomena, to predict phenomena, and to integrate our knowledge of phenomena. If an entity functions in these ways but fails to fit a particular conception of theory structure, this failure counts against the conception of theory structure and not against the status of the entity as a theory. 'Evolutionary theory' functions in these ways. Hence, that it fails to conform to a particular conception of theory structure counts against that conception. I argue that it, like theories of physics, fails to conform to the syntactic conception but conforms very well to the semantic conception. Hence, in a semantic conception, 'evolutionary theory' conforms to both the functional and structural criteria for a genuine scientific theory.

3.1. The Population-Genetical Account of Michael Ruse

In his 1973 book, *The Philosophy of Biology*, Michael Ruse provides a systematic and detailed treatment of the structure of evolutionary theory, the logic of evolutionary explanation, theory reduction in genetics, and teleology. The unifying theme of the book is that biology is not a different kind of science from physics and that the logical empiricist conception of science is the correct conception for both. Ruse takes for granted that the correctness of the logical empiricist conception in the context of physics is well established and accepted. Hence, his task is to establish that biology, in particular evolutionary biology, conforms to the logical empiricist conception of science. By establishing this he will have established that biology and physics conform to the same conception of the logic, epistemology, metaphysics, and methodology of science. A central part of the argument of the book is therefore that evolutionary theory conforms to the syntactic conception of theory structure and that evolutionary explanations are deductive-nomological in form.

Ruse's argument that evolutionary theory conforms to the syntactic conception is two-staged. First, he argues that population genetics is the core of evolutionary theory by which he means that population genetics describes all of the fundamental mechanisms of evolutionary change. Second, he argues that population genetics conforms to the syntactic conception. These two claims together entail that the core of evolutionary theory conforms to the syntactic conception.

For Ruse, population genetics is the core of evolutionary theory because it unifies all evolutionary studies (embryology, systematics, morphology, paleontology, etc.) by being presupposed by them all. The basis for this contention is his view that

> basic to modern evolutionary thought is the claim that the answers to questions about large-scale evolutionary changes are to be found in our knowledge of small-scale changes—changes so small that they would not normally be labelled 'evolutionary'. Modern biologists believe that the organic world which we see around us (and, of which we are part) is indeed the product of a slow, gradual evolutionary process; however, they believe that the process which brings about the largest changes is no more than the long term cumulative effect of processes which bring about the smallest heritable changes. But since population genetics is the science which studies these small changes, we can therefore see its importance for the study of large

changes—the study which is called 'evolutionary theory'. *Population Gene-tics is presupposed by all other evolutionary studies.* (Ruse 1973, p.48)

As can be seen from this quotation, for Ruse, the mechanisms described by population genetic theory are exactly the mechanisms that bring about evolutionary change. Hence, the mechanistic basis of the evolutionary changes that are studied by various branches of evolutionary biology (paleontology, taxonomy, ecology, etc.) are to be found in mechanisms described by population genetics. This argument is extrapolationist in character, that is, it assumes that the causal mechanisms underlying large-scale evolutionary changes can be extrapolated from the causal mechanisms underlying small-scale change because large-scale phenomena are only the cumulative effect of small-scale changes. What follows, quite obviously, from this assumption is that population genetic theory is the core of evolutionary theory. Indeed, it is hard to see why population genetic theory and evolutionary theory are not one and the same theory. Population genetics certainly does not constitute the whole of evolutionary *studies*, but, since a theory is a description of causal mechanisms, population genetic theory does appear, in Ruse's view, to be identical to evolutionary *theory*.

The second stage in Ruse's argument is to establish that population genetic theory conforms to the syntactic conception. The argument here consists of a demonstration that the Hardy-Weinberg law can be deduced from Mendel's first law (the law of segregation) which, along with Mendel's second law (the law of independent assortment), is, according to Ruse, an axiom of Mendelian (population) genetic theory.

The Hardy-Weinberg law is a law of equilibrium which states that, after the first generation, the ratio of alleles at each locus within a population will remain constant unless acted upon by outside forces (for example, selection, mutation, migration) and that the ratio will be

$$p^2 \, A_1A_1 : 2pq \, A_1A_2 : q^2 \, A_2A_2$$

where $p : q$ is the ratio of A_1 alleles to A_2 alleles in the first generation. The derivation of this law from Mendel's second law involves tabulating all the possible outcomes of crossing all the possible pairings of the two alternate alleles with each other (e.g., $A_1A_2 \times A_2A_2, A_1A_1 \times A_1A_1$, etc.). That this tabulation will yield the actual ratio in the next generation in a large random-mating population is guaranteed by Mendel's first law, since in accordance with that law the alleles at a given locus will segregate to form gametes containing only one of the alternate alleles at that locus and will then recombine in the formation of a zygote to produce all of the possible pairwise combinations of individual alleles. This tabulation yields the Hardy-Weinberg equilibrium. That this ratio will remain constant is easily demonstrated by pointing out that the new ratio $p_1 : q_1$ is logically equivalent to the original ratio $p : q$, since

$$p_1 = p^2 + pq = p\,(p + q),\text{ and}$$

$$q_1 = q^2 + pq = q\,(q + p),\text{ hence}$$

$$p_1 : q_1 <-> p\,(p + q) : q\,(q + p) <-> p : q.$$

As with most derivations within a scientific theory in the syntactic conception, this one requires a number of additional assumptions. It requires the assumption that there is no difference between a male-female cross and a female-male cross. It also requires that one assume the axioms of arithmetic, mathematical logic, and Boolean algebra—none of which are among the theorems of the theory. This assumption of other axiomatic systems is an example of the hybrid, inpure nature of the axiomatization of scientific theories in a syntactic conception (see chapter 2, section 2.6).

On the strength of this demonstration, Ruse concludes, "We can now clearly see that at least parts of Mendelian genetic theory are axiomatized" (Ruse 1973, p. 35). This conclusion, in conjunction with his conclusion that population genetic theory is the core of evolutionary theory, entails that at least parts (indeed, the central mechanistic part) of evolutionary theory are axiomatized: "Hence, through the incorporation of population genetics into evolutionary theory there has been an extension of the axiomatic nature of evolutionary theory" (Ruse 1973, p. 65). "My claims in this chapter about evolutionary theory are that I think the theory has an overall unified structure of the form I sketched earlier [population genetics being presupposed by, and hence unifying, all other evolutionary studies], that parts are axiomatized, and there is no theoretical objection to an overall axiomatization" (Ruse 1973, p. 68).

This, to say the least, is a very sketchy and modest attempt at axiomatization. To be fair, however, Ruse does not claim to have given anything like a complete axiomatization. His intention is to demonstrate that axiomatization is, in principle, possible and, at least in part, achievable. The important question is whether such a sketchy account establishes, even weakly, that evolutionary theory conforms to the syntactic conception. But, as I shall argue in section 3.3, more is wrong here than the sketchiness of the argument.

Weak though this demonstration is, Ruse strengthens his overall case that biology conforms to the logical empiricist conception of science by arguing in subsequent chapters that evolutionary explanations conform to the deductive-nomological view of explanation. In addition, he argues, quite convincingly, against the positions of those, like Goudge and Gallie, who argue against the adequacy of the logical empiricist position in the context of biology. Indeed, the cogency of his arguments against his opponents provides that strongest support for his own view. The failure of the positive arguments, however, is not offset by these arguments against alternatives. And even these are weakened by the fact that the semantic conception was not, at the time he wrote his book, among the alternative conceptions to the syntactic conception in the context of biology (though it was in the context of physics). Hence, Ruse provides no argument against this alternative, and he has taken little interest in defending his view against it since its development by Beatty, Lloyd, and myself.

3.2. The Selection Theory Accounts of Mary Williams and Alexander Rosenberg

Unlike Ruse, Mary Williams does undertake to provide a complete axiomatization, although she claims in a later paper (Williams 1973b) that it is a naive axiomatization. It is naive because it is "closer in style to the axiomatizations of Euclid and Newton than to the formal axiomatizations of the Russell-Whitehead school" (Williams 1973b, p. 84). This distinction, I assume, is based on the fact that her axiomatization of evolutionary theory, like many axiomatizations of mathematical theories, is informal, presupposing a theory of inference (usually mthematical logic) and general set theory (see the remarks in chapter 2 section 2.6 about informal theories).

Quite clearly, Williams's axiomatization presupposes a theory of inference and general set theory: that is, both theories are required by her axiomatization, but the theorems of neither are among the theorems of evolutionary theory in her axiomatization. This, however, is what one would expect to be the case for any axiomatization of a scientific theory, since a formal axiomatization that included as theorems of the axiomatized scientific theory all the theorems of set theory, geometry, and so forth, would be of so great a complexity as to make the task incapable of completion. As indicated in chapter 2, the need to presuppose general set theory in any axiomatization, in a syntactic conception, provides a substantial reason for favoring a semantic conception approach to formalizing scientific theories—but more of this in the next chapter.

What Williams offers is an axiomatization of the theory of natural selection and not, as Ruse attempts to offer, population genetic theory. Also unlike Ruse, she is not primarily interested in establishing that evolutionary theory conforms to the syntactic conception of theory structure. She takes for granted the applicability and appropriateness of the syntactic conception and provides a formalization within it which demonstrates the richness of formalization in evolutionary biology. She also takes for granted that an axiomatization of selection theory is an axiomatization of evolutioanry theory.

This assumption, as Rosenberg quite clearly sees, is crucial to establishing that evolutionary theory conforms to the syntactic conception of theory structure. In order for her exercise in axiomatization to be taken as establishing that *evolutionary theory* conforms to the syntactic conception, one would have to establish that an axiomatization of selection theory constitutes an axiomatization of evolutionary theory. This, indeed, is exactly what Rosenberg attempts to do. His defence of Williams's axiomatization and his employment of it in his characterization of evolutionary theory contain a quite explicit argument for the conclusion that selection theory and evolutionary theory are one in the same theory. In effect, he argues that mechanisms of heredity are part of the causal framework within which evolutionary change is possible but that they are not among the actual mechanisms which are causally responsible for evolutionary change within this framework. The mechanisms of selection, however, are causally responsible for evolutionary change. Hence, since the mechanisms of selection are the mechanisms of evolution, selection theory and evolutionary theory are one and the same theory. This conclusion, combined with a demonstration that selection theory conforms to the syntactic conception, entails that evolutionary theory conforms to the syntactic conception. A more detailed analysis of his argument is given below.

Williams's axiomatization is impressive. Indeed, it is probably the best example of the axiomatic method applied to a biological theory: considerably more impressive than Woodger's earlier attempts. What it quite clearly shows is the nature of the axiomatization of scientific theories, and it demonstrates the enormous benefits of formalization in science—benefits that, I argue, can also be obtained by formalization in a semantic conception.

Williams's axiomatization consists of the following:[2]

(1) Two primitive terms: *biological entity* and *is a parent of*

(2) Definitions of other terms (e.g., *ancestor, clan, subclan*) in terms of these primitives and set-theoretical principles

(3) Two axioms stating general propositions that are true of all evolutionary theories:

    (i) No biological entity is a parent of itself.

    (ii) If a is an ancestor of b then b is not an ancestor of a.

(4) An operational definition of fitness

(5) Five axioms of Darwinian evolutionary theory:

    1. Every Darwinian subclan is a subclan.

2. There is an upper limit to the number of biological entities in any generation of a Darwinian clan.

3. For each biological entity, there is a positive and real number that describes its fitness in a particular environment.

4. If (a) any Darwinian subclan, D, has a subcland D_1, and (b) D_2 is superior in fitness to the rest of D for sufficiently many generations, then the proportion of D_1 in D will increase.

5. In every generation of a Darwinian subcland D (that is not on the verge of extinction), there is a subcland, D_1; and D_1 is superior in fitness to the rest of D for long enough to ensure that D_1 will increase relative to D; and as long as D_1 is not fixed in D, it retains sufficient superiority to ensure further increases relative to D.

3.3. The Insights and Inadequacies of These Accounts

What is immediately obvious about these two accounts is that they differ over the exact nature of evolutionary theory. Ruse equates evolutionary theory with population genetic theory, and Williams and Rosenberg equate it with selection theory. As will emerge from the following discussion, Ruse and Rosenberg each have arguments for equating evolutionary theory with their respective core theory. What I contend is that most of their arguments actually demonstrate that evolutioanry theory is a composite of both of their core theories and more, and not, therefore, one or the other. Although there are interconnections between the views of Ruse and of Williams and Rosenberg, I shall, for the most part, discuss them separately, beginning with Ruse's views.

There are several problems with Ruse's conception of the structure of evolutionary theory: a conception which is crucial to the success of even the limited case he makes for its axiomatic-deductive character. First, it is not at all clear that Ruse has correctly identified the axioms of evolutionary theory. Even if one takes for granted that Mendel's laws are appropriate axioms for population genetics, it does not follow that they are appropriate axioms for evolutionary theory. Indeed, quite the opposite appears to be the case.

As John Beatty has argued (Beatty 1981; see also Rosenberg 1985, pp. 134–136), Mendel's laws cannot serve as axioms of a formalization in mathematical logic of evolutionary theory because Mendel's laws are themselves an outcome of the evolutionary process. In other words, the fact that organisms evolved in such a way that information is transmitted from generation to generation in accordance with Mendel's laws is a phenomenon that is in need of evolutionary explanation. As was clear from the exposition of Ruse's arguments given above, Mendel's laws assume, among a host of other things, sexually reproducing populations in which male-female and female-male crosses are equivalent in results and male-male and female-female crosses do not occur. In cases of asexual reproduction, Mendel's laws do not describe hereditary processes. Of course, there may be excellent grounds for thinking that sexual reproduction in accordance with Mendel's laws is exactly what one would expect given evolutionary theory: that is, one might well be able to explain, and perhaps even predict, the emergence of sexually reproducing populations given modern evolutionary theory and biochemistry. However, what this possibility makes clear is that heredity in accordance with Mendel's laws is something that calls for an evolutionary explanation. Hence, heredity in accordance with Mendel's laws must, in Ruse's hypothetical-deductive view of science, be deducible from the axioms of evolutioary theory. And, since laws that must be deducible from evolutionary theory can hardly serve as axioms of evolutionary theory, Mendel's laws cannot serve as axioms of evolutionary theory.

More is at stake here than just a misidentification of the axioms of evolutionary theory. In Ruse's view, population genetics is the theory that describes the processes of small-scale changes and evolution is just the cumulative effect of small changes. Hence, as outlined in section 3.1 above, population genetics is, for Ruse, the core of evolutionary theory because it describes the processes (mechanisms) of evolutionary change: that is, population genetics is not just a component in a complex which constitutes evolutionary theory. Population genetics (as his often reproduced diagram, Ruse 1973, p. 49, shows) is the principal component. In fact, Ruse argues at length against Beckner's view that it is one among many components. Given this understanding of the place of population genetics within evolutionary theory (a place which effectively identifies evolutionary *theory*, in contrast to evolutionary studies, with population genetic theory), Ruse is clearly committed to holding that the axioms of population genetics (for Ruse, Mendel's laws) are the axioms of evolutionary theory. Hence, Beatty's argument, which demonstrates that Mendel's laws cannot be axioms of evolutioary theory, entails that either Ruse has incorrectly identified the axioms of population genetics or that Ruse's position on the centrality of population genetics is incorrect.

Of course, it could be that Mendel's laws are not among the axioms of population genetic theory and that a correctly identified set of axioms would be such that an evolutionary explanation of why heredity occurs in accordance with them was not required. Were this the case, Ruse's claim that population genetic theory is the core of evolutionary theory would be untouched by Beatty's criticism.

I have three comments on this possibility. First, it is difficult to take this possibility seriously, since it is widely held that some formulation of Mendel's laws is among the axioms of population genetic theory. In addition, an alternative set of axioms that does not contain some formulation of Mendel's laws (not to mention a set that does contain axioms that are not in need of an evolutionary explanation) has not even been suggested, let alone developed.

Second, Beatty's argument is implicitly generic: that is, although his argument is formulated in terms of Mendel's laws, the thrust of the argument is that *any* system of heredity will be an evolved system, and hence in need of an evolutionary explanation. The generic argument can be simply stated. Organisms are the product of evolution. Hence, the method by which they reproduce is a product of evolution. Hence, laws describing the mechanisms of reproduction, which will include the biological transmission of biological information, are describing an evolved system. Therefore, these laws cannot be axioms of a theory of evolution. Rosenberg explicitly makes a similar generic argument.

Third, even if, notwithstanding the first two points, a set of axioms for population genetic theory could be formulated such that no formulation of Mendel's laws was a member and only laws that did not need an evolutionary explanation were members, Ruse's argument would nonetheless be seriously undermined. The second stage of Ruse's argument involves a demonstration that the Hardy-Weinberg law can be deduced from Mendel's laws. If Mendel's laws are axioms of population genetic theory and if population genetic theory is the core of evolutioary theory, then Ruse, with some credibility, can claim to have demonstrated in a sketchy way, that evolutionary theory is axiomatic-deductive in character. If Mendel's laws are not among the axioms of population genetic theory, his demonstration, though interesting as an exercise in deduction, fails to demonstrate anything about evolutionary theory.

The second problem with Ruse's view of the structure of evolutionary theory is the questionable assumption that evolution is the result of the accumulation of small changes. This gradualist, extrapolationist assumption is crucial to Ruse's argument that population genetics is the core of evolutionary theory. Given the importance of this assumption to the argument, it is worth quoting again the argument here to highlight the centrality of this assumption:

> Basic to modern evolutionary thought is the claim that the answers to questions about large-scale evolutionary changes are to be found in our knowledge of small-scale changes—changes so small that they would not normally be labelled 'evolutionary'. Modern biologists believe that the organic world which we see around us (and, of which we are part) is indeed the product of a slow, gradual evolutionary process; however, they believe that the process which brings about the largest changes is no more than the long term cumulative effect of processes which bring about the smallest heritable changes. But

since population genetics is the science which studies these small changes, we can therefore see its importance for the study of large changes—the study which is called 'evolutionary theory'.

The tenability of this assumption, however, has been vigorously attacked during the last decade, most notably by Niles Eldredge and Stephen Gould in a number of papers (Eldredge and Gould 1972; Gould and Eldredge 1977; Gould 1980a, 1980b, 1981, 1982; Eldredge 1985a, 1985b). And, although I do not accept the more general conclusion contained in a number of papers that the modern synthetic theory is inadequate to explain certain evolutionary phenomena (see Thompson 1983a and 1988b) I think their case for rejecting the pervasiveness in the evolutionary thinking of this gradualist, extrapolationist assumption is cogent (see also Stebbins and Ayala 1981; Orzack 1981; White 1981).

In essence, Eldredge, Gould, and, by 1980, a host of other biologists hold that evolution was not always gradual, was not always a result of selection, and was not always explainable in terms of microevolutionary processes (that is, population genetics). They hold that there is clear evidence that evolution was marked by long periods of stasis punctuated by sudden events of speciation and that any adequate explanation of this pattern requires reference to mechanisms of rapid genetic revolutions which are not immediately under the control of selection and to mechanisms of selection above the level of populations.

Gould, one of the strongest advocates of this new view, argued initially for the extreme position that the need to refer to these nongradual, nonextrapolationist mechanisms entails that the modern synthesis is dead or at least in need of substantial revision. He held that punctuated equilibrium offers a new and more general *theory* of evolution—indeed, he claimed that it offers a new pardigm. As I have argued (Thompson 1983a, 1988b), this extreme position is unwarranted, no matter how viable the rejection of a gradualist, extrapolationist position like Ruse's might be.

Ruse, following George Gaylord Simpson (1953) and Ernst Mayr (1963), characterized the modern synthesis in extremely narrow terms. Gould is correct when he challenges this narrow interpretation, and it might be well to dispense with the name *modern synthesis* in order to avoid confusion with this narrow exposition of its character. Gould is not correct, however, in his claim that a new theory has been offered, and he is grossly exaggerating when he claims that a new paradigm has been presented. At best, punctuated equilibria corrects an undue emphasis on gradualism, extrapolationism, and selectionism. All the examples of new mechanisms offered by Gould are, as I have argued, within the scope of evolutionary theory as expounded by Maynard Smith, Stebbins, Mettler and Gregg, and numerous other evolutionary biologists, all of whose expositions have been widely used as texts for several decades. The characterization of evolution offered by these writers includes discussions of all but one of Gould's proposed new mechanisms (species selection). And, as I have argued, all of Gould's mechanisms fall within the scope of one or more of the theories of genetics, ecology, selection, or embryology. And since, as I maintain, evolutionary theory is a composite of these theoretical systems, evolutionary theory can encompass all of Gould's and Eldredge's mechanisms. The integration of these systems is by no means complete, but the general character is clear. It is the interactive nature of these theoretical systems that makes possible explanations of evolutionary change of the kind Gould and Eldredge describe.

The problem Ruse faces, then, is that the assumption of extrapolationism (though perhaps not gradualism, since the founder effect is population genetical even though rapid) is central to his conception of evolutionary theory: that is, if population genetics constitutes the mechanistic core of evolutioary theory, then large-scale events must be the result (cumulative effect) of population-genetical-level changes. If, as quite clearly seems to be the case, evolution can be the result of chromosomal inversions (see White 1968, 1978), selection above the level of the individual (see Sober 1981, 1984b; Sober and Lewontin 1982), and so forth, then mechanisms other than those described by population genetics will need to be employed in explaining evolution. Hence, large-scale evolutionary changes cannot, in many instances, be explained by reference to the mechanisms described by population genetics alone or by reference to the cumulative effect (extrapolations) of the operation of those mechanisms over time. Therefore, population genetics cannot be the mechanistic core of evolutionary theory. Hence, although it is a very important part of evolutionary theory, it is nonetheless only one of the theories that together constitute an evolutionary theoretical framework.

The implication of this for Ruse's demonstration that evolutionary theory is axiomatic-deductive in logical structure is that a central premise in the argument is false: that is, population genetics is not the mechanistic core of the theory. And, this has far-reaching consequences. This premise is essential to Ruse's argument because in a syntactic view the theory being formalized must be a unified deductive structure. If evolutionary theory is in fact identical to population genetic theory, then evolutionary theory can be formalized in a syntactic conception because population genetic theory can be shown to be a unified deductive structure. If, however, evolutionary theory is a composite of population genetic theory, cytological theory, and so forth, then it fails to have the unified deductive structure required to provide a syntactic account.

A third problem with Ruse's view focuses on the degree to which even his modest example of the deductive character of population genetics represents a true instance of a deduction. In many respects the Hardy-Weinberg law is an instance, or perhaps a part of the meaning, of Mendel's first law rather than a deduction from it in the sense of an inference according to the transformation rules of mathematical logic. Mendel's first law, the law of segregation, as formulated by Ruse, is as follows:

M1:   For each sexual individual, each parent contributes one and only one of the genes at every locus. These genes come from the corresponding loci in the parents, and the chance of any parental gene being transmitted is the same as the chance of the other gene at the same parental locus.[3]

What this *means* is that offspring have one and only one gene from each parent at each locus and that all possible gene pairs are equally likely: that is, Mendel's first law *defines* the hereditary transmission of genes at a particular locus as a Cartesian product of the two parental sets of genes at the corresponding parental loci. All the Hardy-Weinberg law does is to *state* the Cartesian product, under abstract mating frequencies, which Mendel's law *defines*. And even though, in some formal sense, statements specifying the meaning of a claim or spelling out the nature of a defined state of affairs are deductions from that claim or definition, such deductions are trivial and hardly constitute the kind of significant deductions believed to be characteristic of theories as axiomatic-deductive structures.

Consider, for example, Newton's third law:

N3: for every action there is an equal and opposite reaction.

What this law *means* is that for any force of magnitude x, there is a corresponding force of magnitude x such that the vector addition of the forces equals 0. In other words, Newton's third law *defines* a mechanical system as a balanced force system. A law stating that

for any force $(F_1 + F_2)$ there is a force $-(F_1 + F_2)$

merely states what Newton's third law defines under conditions of combined vector forces. It is, in effect, one instance of Newton's third law (arithmetic is presupposed as part of the context within which the theory is formulated). And, although this is in a trivial sense a deduction, it is not an example of the deduction of a lower-level law of Newtonian mechanics. It is the weakest kind of deduction possible and only establishes that something follows from every claim and not that all the significant claims of a scientific theory follow from other claims and ultimately from the axioms of the theory.

A final example: the claim "No married man is a bachelor" does in a formal sense follow deductively from the claim "All bachelors are unmarried males." But this deduction is trival by comparison with the deduction of

Galileo's law from Newton's second law. Consequently, what Ruse appears to have offered is not just a very sketchy demonstration of the deductive nature of Mendelian genetics but merely a trivial and inconsequential unpacking of the meaning of Mendel's first law—that is, of the Cartesian product implicit in the law.

These problems with Ruse's demonstration are extremely damaging to his position; they undermine crucial elements in his argument. The upshot of the first two problems is that Ruse's identification of evolutionary theory with population genetic theory is untenable. Other difficulties with this identification are discussed below in the context of Williams's and Rosenberg's attempt to identify evolutionary theory with selection theory. I now turn to a discussion of the problems with that attempt.

Elliot Sober and Michael Ruse have both criticized Mary Williams's axiomatization. Sober (Sober 1984a, pp. 372–383, 1984b, pp. 188–196) points out that axiomatization contains no source laws; does not mention mutation, migration, systems of mating, and numerous other causes of evolution which evolutionary biology takes into account; excludes genetics; and is Malthusian, that is, incorrectly makes selection dependent on reproductive rates. Ruse (Ruse 1973, p. 50; and especially 1977, pp. 111–113) also criticizes Williams's axiomatization for making no reference to genetics. This is the important criticism relative to the thesis of this book.

In essence, Ruse's argument is that Williams's axiomatization is inadequate as an axiomatization of evolutionary theory because it contains no hereditary mechanism. Ruse correctly contends that any adequate characterization of evolutionary theory must take account of three central features: variation, natural selection (that is, nonrandom differential reproduction, which is a function of the variation that maps the entire population into the subset of reproductively successful members of the entire population), and heredity (that is, the transmission to offspring of parental characteristics). Natural selection can occur in the absence of heritability of characteristics (as indicated in chapter 1), but evolution cannot, since, without heritability, natural selection will have no causal effect on subsequent generations. Hence, the absence of a hereditary mechanism renders Williams's axiomatization inadequate as an axiomatization of evolutionary theory regardless of one's views about its status as an axiomatizaiton of the theory of natural selection. Moreover, Ruse thinks that there is no satisfactory way to incorporate an account of heredity into her axiomatization.

Ruse, on the other hand, considers his own axiomatization sketch to be conceptually adequate because it incorporates all three of the above features by identifying population genetics as the core of evolutionary theory. In the first place, population genetics quite obviously provides a theory of heritability. Second, it provides an account of variation and natural selection in terms of allelic frequencies. Variation within a population is a result of high frequency of polymorphic loci (loci with two or more alternate alleles). This high level is maintained by mutation, recombination, immigration, balancing selection, and so forth. Natural selection is a function which maps one set of allelic frequencies into a temporally later set of allelic frequencies and can be expressed in the theory as coefficients of selection. In this view, evolution is a nonrandom cumulative change in allelic frequencies.

Recently Alexander Rosenberg has defended Williams's account and criticized Ruse's account (Rosenberg 1985). Rosenberg considers it a strength of Williams's account that it is neutral on the question of hereditary mechanisms and a defect in Ruse's account that it is so wedded to a particular theory of heredity. He argues that evolutionary theory is not dependent on any particular theory of heredity and that, far from being the core of evolutionary theory, a theory of heredity is simply an assumption of the theory. The central mechanism of evolution is natural selection. Heredity is assumed as a background condition, albeit an important one. Hence, the theory of evolution is neutral on hereditary mechanisms.

According to Rosenberg, since Ruse's account is not only not neutral with regard to the mechanism of heredity—it is entirely dependent on current population genetic theory—but also characterizes evolutionary theory entirely in terms of heredity, it misrepresents the character of the theory. Williams's account, on the other hand, has precisely the neutrality concerning hereditary mechanisms that is required, as well as the correct emphasis on the centrality of natural selection. Rosenberg also argues that population genetics cannot be the core of evolutionary theory because laws like Mendel's laws and the Hardy-Weinberg law do not describe situations of change but situations of equilibrium. In addition to the laws of Mendelian genetics, evolution requires laws that disrupt the equilibrium described by Mendelian genetics. Indeed, the mechanisms of evolutionary change are those that disrupt the equilibrium. Hence, evolutionary theory, properly understood, describes mechanisms that disrupt this equilibrium.

These two arguments of Rosenberg against Ruse's claim that Mendelian genetics is the core of evolutionary theory have considerable merit (they constitute two more problems with Ruse's position). Rosenberg is correct: no particular theory of heredity is required by evolutionary theory. All that is required is that characteristics of parents be transmittable to offspring. He is also correct that natural selection is a prime mechanism without which population genetic theory would predict a situation of almost complete stasis—the only changes being due to random drift and recombination. A further problem (not mentioned by Rosenberg) with Ruse's position comes into focus when the role of natural selection in evolutionary change is examined. It is clear that natural selection usually acts on phenotypes and not directly on genotypes. Therefore, contrary to Ruse's position, it is not accurately represented by selection co-efficients in a genetic calculus.

Despite all of this, however, Rosenberg's detaching of heredity from evolutionary theory is untenable for the same reasons given by Ruse and Sober for rejecting the adequacy of Williams's axiomatization of current evolutionary theory. That population genetics is not by itself sufficient to entail evolutionary change does not entail that it is not a central part of evolutionary theory. Natural selection by itself also does not entail evolutionary change, since the effects of selection, without heredity, are limited to each generation and cannot be perpetuated or accumulated. What these arguments for individual insufficiency show is that both are essential. An adequate evolutionary theoretical framework, as argued above, is a composite of, among other theories, theories of both heredity and natural selection. And, despite Rosenberg's praise of neutrality on the question of hereditary mechanisms, this composite nature is not undermined by the unlikely possiblity that our current account of the specific mechanisms is wrong. To claim that evolutionary theory presupposes *some* hereditary mechanism but not any specific mechanism does not entail that heredity is not an essential component in any *theory* about evolution.

A consideration of the similar situation of natural selection makes this point clear: that is, it is also true that evolutionary theory presupposes *some* mechanisms of selection but not any specific mechanisms—though unlikely, balancing selection, diversifying selection, and so on may be incorrect specific mechanisms of selection even though some mechanisms of selection are among the principle causes of evolution. This is not—as it should not be—taken by Rosenberg, however, to entail that natural selection is not an essential component of the theory. Both natural selection and heredity are essential components of the theory even though no specific account of the mechanism of natural selection or heredity may be entirely correct and hence essential to the theory. What seems clear is that some—perhaps yet unformulated—account of both must be possible. Were it the case that, in principle, no account could be given of one or the other of heredity and selection, current evolutionary theory would, in principle, be incapable of formulation. And this point demonstrates the degree to which both components are essential to the theory.[4]

Moreover, Rosenberg's argument for detaching heredity from evolutionary theory, on the basis of his contention that population genetic theory entails only stasis, is also not compelling. Rosenberg is quite correct that, within a Darwinian evolutionary framework, natural selection is the prime force which disturbs the genetic equilibrium expressed in the population-genetic Hardy-Weinberg law. He is wrong, however, to see this as entailing that natural selection theory is the theory that describes the actual mechanisms of evolution. Consider Newton's first law of motion:

N1:   Every body tends to remain in a state of rest or uniform motion unless acted upon by an external unbalanced force.

This law, like the Hardy-Weinberg law, states, in effect, that if nothing happens then nothing will happen. It is a law of equilibrium. Of course, if something happens, then the equilibrium will be disturbed in both cases: that is, if an external unbalanced force does act on a body, the body will undergo a change in velocity. Similarly, if uncompensated selection takes place in a population, the ratio of alleles at the loci affected by the selective force will undergo a change. However, that Newton's first law is a law of equilibrium does not in any way entail that it is not a part (indeed, an essential part) of Newtonian mechanical theory.

What emerges from this discussion is that Ruse's account identifies evolutionary theory with a theory of heredity, whereas Williams's account identifies evolutionary theory with a theory of natural selection, and both of these identifications misrepresent evolutionary theory. It is a composite of both and more. The two accounts also demonstrate the difficulty of providing a single axiomatization of this composite structure.

The main difficulty is that an evolutionary theoretical framework is a family of interacting theories rather than a unified structure. Consequently, a syntactic conception formalization of the theory, insofar as it is possible and desirable, can only be provided for the component theoretical frameworks and not for the theory as a whole. Therefore, as one would expect, this component axiomatization is precisely what Williams and Ruse, by necessity, have provided.

What emerges, then, is that a conception of theory structure that is faithful to the actual structure of the Darwinian evolutionary theoretical framework will be one that permits the theory of natural selection and the theory of heredity—at present population genetic theory—along with other theories to be separately formalized but capable of interaction and simultaneous employment under those formalizations.

Notes

1. I am grateful to Wim van der Steen for making me aware of the confusion that might arise from the use of *evolutionary theory* to refer to the quite different accounts of Ruse, Williams and Rosenberg, and myself. Although far from ideal, I hope the convention I have adopted will avoid confusion and will not be too tedious.

2. An excellent exposition of Williams's axiomatization can be found in Rosenberg 1985, and a simplified version by Williams can be found in Williams 1973a.

3. There are a multitude of different formulations of this law. All state the same essential facts as Ruse's formulation, and, more significantly, all *mean* the same thing. For example, Rosenberg states the law as follows:

M1:   In sexual species, each parent contributes one gene at each locus, and the probability of an offspring's having genes from one parent at a locus is equal to the probability of having a gene from the other parent at that locus.

4. Rosenberg has advanced another argument which, though undermining the claim that population genetics is the core of evolutionary theory, is entirely uncompeling as an argument against considering heredity as an essential component in evolutionary theory. He has argued that heredity is a presupposition of any evolutionary theory and not just of Darwinian evolutionary theory. Without debating the truth of this claim, I fail to see how, even if true, it entails that it is not an essential part of current Darwinian evolutionary theory. It is like claiming that since oxygen is an ingredient in all cases of combustion and not just those involving the burning of a candle, it is not an essential part of the burning of a candle. I see no contradiction in claiming that something is presupposed by all theories of a given type and is an essential ingredient in any specific theory of that type.

CHAPTER 4

The Semantic Conception of Theory Structure

I turn now to the semantic conception of theories. This conception has a relatively short history. Quite early formulations were suggested by Evert Beth (a state space approach) in 1948–49 (Beth 1948, 1949; see also 1961) and by Patrick Suppes (a set-theoretical predicate approach) in 1957 in his *Introduction to Logic* (Suppes 1957).

Suppes suggested that scientific theories are more appropriately formalized as set-theoretical predicates. Shortly thereafter Robert Stoll, in his *Set Theory and Logic* (1963), made a similar claim about the formalizaiton of informal theories of which scientific theories are instances. Suppes wrote a number of papers during the 1960s indicating the features of theories that were better represented on a set-theoretical predicate conception of theories (see, for example, Suppes 1962). And in 1967 he wrote a brief, nontechnical account of his view. In this paper he quite clearly sets out his reasons for rejecting the "standard sketch of scientific theories" (the syntactic conception) and for adopting a semantic conception. His central thesis is that scientific theories are not appropriately or usefully formalized as axiomatizations in mathematical logic but rather in set theory.

The main thrust of his argument is that correspondence rules (he calls them "coordinating definitions") "do not in the sense of modern logic provide an adequate semantics for the formal calculus [formal system]" (Suppes 1967, p. 57). One should instead talk about models of theory. These models are nonlinguistic entities that are highly abstract and far removed from the empirical phenomena to which they will be applied. This, as will emerge below, is one of the major strengths of this conception, since it makes intelligible, indeed necessary, the actual use of a hierarchy of theories in the application of the theory to phenomena.

Suppes suggests two reasons why the syntactic view is so widely held, despite what he argues are its logical and practical weaknesses. First, philosophers' examples of scientific theories are usually fairly simple and therefore easily able to be given a linguistic formualtion. Not surprisingly, most examples used to explicate and defend the syntactic view are drawn from Newtonian mechanics—and from a reasonably simple and sketchy account of it.

Also not surprisingly, the advocates of the semantic view discuss complex theories such as quantum mechanics (see van Fraassen 1972), learning theory (see Suppes 1962), and evolutionary theory (see Beatty 1980a, 1980b; Lloyd 1983, 1984, 1986, 1987; Thompson 1983b, 1985, 1986, 1987, 1988a). Second, there is a much more sophisticated mathematical character to discussions of models of a theory than to discussions of correspondence rules (coordinating definitions).

During the 1970s a large number of philosophers from a variety of perspectives advocated and defended the semantic conception (see, for example Suppe 1967, 1972a, 1972b, 1974, 1976; van Fraassen 1970, 1972, 1980; Sneed 1971; Stegmuller 1976). In subsequent sections of this chapter I discuss two alternative approaches to theory structure within the semantic conception: the set-theoretical approach of Suppes and the state space approach of van Fraassen, which is an extension of Beth's semantics of physical theories and of Suppe's similar view, which he independently developed (Suppe 1967). Not discussed is the structuralist approach of Sneed and Stegmuller. Those who wish some acquaintance with this approach will find the expositions and reviews of Raimo Tuolema (1978) and Werner Diederich (1982) extremely informative. I decided not to discuss this approach largely because of the quite different character of, as well as motivation for (see Suppe 1979, p. 322), this approach compared with the set-theoretical and state space approaches, which have much in common with each other and have dominated discussions in the context of biology. Hence, the structuralist approach would have stood very isolated, since it does not play any role in the discussions in chapter 5, 6, and 7.

During the 1980s John Beatty, Elizabeth Lloyd, and I have been extending and applying the semantic conception in the context of biology and, in particular, in the context of evolutionary theory and genetics.

4.1. Models of Formal Systems

The concept of a 'model' plays an extremely important role in the two versions of the semantic conception of scientific theories that are discussed in this chapter. Hence, I shall very briefly discuss, in this section, the concept of 'model' as it is used in connection with the semantic conception. The details of its role and the importance of that role will emerge in the following sections. The purpose of this section is to make clear in general terms the meaning of 'model'.

The term *model* has a multitude of different meanings within scientific, mathematical, and philosophical discourse. For example, sometimes *model* can refer to an experimental replication in the laboratory of a complex set of phenomena. The model, in this sense, enables the researcher to control parameters that could not be controlled in nature. Another sense of *model* is an analogical model such as the model of the atom as analogous to the solar system, or electricity to balls moving in a tube. The sense of *model* as it is used in the discussion of the semantic conception of the structure of scientific theories is the sense used in formal semantics: that is, a model is an entity that satisfies an axiomatic structure and by so doing provides an interpretation for that structure. A model satisfies an axiomatic structure if it renders the theorems of the structure true (see section 2.2 for an example based on Riemannian and Euclidean geometry).

Hence, a model for a formal system, in this sense, is a mathematical entity in which all of the theorems of the formal system are true. One can only talk of truth within a model, since a formal system has no meaning and hence the concept of 'truth' is inapplicable. The exact nature of a model in a set-theoretical predicate and in a state space approach can be more easily explicated in the context of the discussion of these approaches and therefore will be dealt with in later sections of this chapter.

4.2. Theories as Specifications of a Class of Models

The semantic conception is so called because scientific theories are conceptualized in terms of models of formal systems (semantic structures); hence, an adequate formal approach to the stucture of science theories consists in the specification of the models of a formal system (that is, the semantics) and not in the specification of a linguistic axiomatic-deductive system (that is, a syntax). The significant differences, therefore, between syntactic and semantic accounts are the nature of an adequate semantics of a scientific theory and the nature of an adequate (logically and heuristically) formalizaiton of a scientific theory. In the syntactic conception, the semantics of a theory are provided by correspondence rules. In a semantic conception, the semantics of a theory is provided directly by defining a class of models. For Suppes, the class of models is directly defined by defining a set-theoretical predicate. For van Fraassen and Suppe, the class of models is defined in terms of a phase space or state space (a topological structure). One point of difference between van Fraassen and Suppe is that van Fraassen identifies theories with state spaces (phase spaces) whereas Suppe understands state spaces as "canonical iconic models of theories" (Suppe 1972a, p. 161, note 18) or "canonical mathematical replicas of theories" (Suppe 1977, pp. 227–228, note 565). In the latter reference Suppe provides reasons for preferring his view to van Fraassen's. Even though Suppe's contention that his view is preferable because it allows the semantic conception to be extended to the analysis of qualitative theories with nonmeasurable parameters is compelling, I shall follow van Fraassen because it makes the exposition of the state space view simpler. In addition, recasting van Fraassen's view, when appropriate, in terms of Suppe's view is reasonably straightforward.

One of the major consequences of the differences in the semantics of the syntactic and semantic conceptions is that the class of models, directly specified in terms of set theory or a state space, is an extralinguistic, highly abstract entity which is most often quite removed from the phenomena to which it is intended to apply. The relationship of a model to phenomena is one of isomorphism, and the establishment of the isomorphism is a complex task not specified by the theory. If the asserted isomorphism is not established, it may be that the theory has no empirical *application*. The theory will nonetheless be empirically *meaningful* (it is a semantic—meaning—structure) in that one knows from the theory what the structure and behavior of phenomena would be if the phenomena were isomorphic to the theory (see Thompson 1987). Hence, in the semantic conception, the empirical meaning of a theory is separate from the empirical application of a theory.[1]

In the syntactic conception, on the other hand, the semantics is provided by correspondence rules which are part of the theory and which directly link the formal system to the phenomenal world. In effect the correspondence rules define an empirical model of the formal system. That empirical model is understood as logically equivalent to the phenomenal system to which the theory applies.

It is for this reason that actual phenomena can be deduced from the statements of the theory: that is, the statements of the theory are laws that describe the *actual* behavior of objects in the world. Hence, any behavior deduced from the statements of the theory is either a prediction about what *actually* will happen under the specified circumstances or an explanation of what *actually* did happen under the specified circumstances. The interpreted formal system directly describes the behavior of entities in the world.

In a semantic conception, a theory (model) is a mathematical entity and is not defined by reference to a formal system. In other words, although a formal system for which the theory could be a model can be constructed, the theory (model) is not constructed as an interpretation of a formal system.[2] It is defined directly by specifying the behavior of a system. And, most importantly, laws do not describe the behavior of objects in the world; they specify the nature and behavior of an abstract system. This abstract system, independently of its specification, is claimed to be isomorphic to a particular empirical system. Establishing this isomorphism requires the employment of a range of other scientific theories and the adoption of theories of methodology (such as theories of experimental design and goodness of fit). None of these theories are part of, or specified by, the scientific theory which is claimed to be isomorphic to a particular empirical system.

As can be seen, despite the differences, the syntactic and semantic conceptions are somewhat interconnected. For any theory directly defined in terms of set theory or a state space, one or more axiomatic-deductive structures (formal systems) could be provided such that the theory is an interpretation of those structures (see note 2). Similarly, for any axiomatic-deductive structure a model could be constructed which would be a highly abstract mathematical entity. This fact has caused some critics of the semantic conception to argue that there is no logical difference between the two conceptions (see, for example, Worrall 1984). In an article several years ago (Thompson 1985), I conceded that there is no genuine *incompatibility* between the two views. The central differences, I claimed, were heuristic and methodological. This position, I now think, underestimates the difference between the two views. The fundamental logical difference is in the way in which the semantics is provided.

Although it is true that for any model one or more formal systems can be constructed which the model satisfies and that for any formal system an abstract mathematical model that satisfies it can be constructed, this interconnectedness breaks down in the context of the structure of scientific theories. The key to the breakdown is found in the relationship of a theory to the world. In a syntactic conception, this relationship is specified by correspondence rules. They provide the semantics for the axiomatic-deductive structure (formal system) and thereby produce a model which is not a highly abstract mathematical entity but a linguistic structure—a deductively related set of statements (laws). Clearly one could provide, for any formal system, an abstract mathematical model, but this is not in fact what correspondence rules do—they provide a linguistic structure. The nature of the semantics for each view is different, and hence the interpreted systems that result are very different. And, were one to attempt to solve this problem by claiming that a scientific theory is a formal system which is interpreted by a highly abstract mathematical model which is, in turn, related to the world by means of a complex hierarchy of other theories, it would become clear that the formal system serves no useful role logically, heuristically, or methodologically. This is so because the model can be defined directly, and more straightforwardly, without any reference to the formal system. And the heuristic and methodological aspects center around the model and its relationship to the empirical world, and not around the formal system.

This is, in essence, the substance of the difference between the two conceptions. The semantic conception calls into question the possiblity of providing an adequate semantics for a scientific theory by means of correspondence rules. It also calls into question the need for any reference to a formal system, since the semantics can be provided directly by defining a mathematical model. In addition to these challenges, advocates of the semantic view have seen the separation, which exists in a semantic conception, of the theory and the method of its application as a major heuristic and methodological advantage of the conception.

Before moving to an exposition of two versions of a semantic conception, I want to emphasize one important similarity between the syntactic and semantic conceptions. They are both conceptions of the formal structure of theories. There is no comfort to be found in the semantic conception for those philosophers who dispute the appropriateness and usefulness of formalization in one or all branches of science. Those of us who espouse the semantic conception are, like those who espouse the syntactic conception, committed to the value of formalization in science and the philosophy of science. Indeed, Patrick Suppes provides the clearest statement of the fact that the semantic conception is a conception of the correct and most useful *formalization* of scientific theories:

> The sense of formalization I shall use in the subsequent discussion is just that of a standard set-theoretical formulation. I do not want to mean by formalization the stricter conception of a first-order theory that assumes only elementary logic. Such stricter formalization is appropriate for the intensive study of many elementary domains of mathematics, but in almost all areas of science a rich mathematical apparatus is needed. We can properly appeal to that apparatus within a set-theoretical framework. (Suppes 1968, p. 653)

The paper from which this quotation is drawn extols the virtues of formalization in the sense set out in the quotation.

4.3. The Set-Theoretical Approach

Patrick Suppes' conception of the structure of scientific theories is a semantic conception because he takes theories to be formalized by defining a set-theoretic predicate which, in effect, defines a class of models. For him a theory is axiomatized by defining a predicate in terms of the concepts of set theory. The result is a set-theoretical predicate which defines a system. Models of the theory are set-theoretical entities which satisfy the set-theoretical predicate and, in the context of scientific theories, are therefore systems which satisfy the set-theoretical predicate. Two models will be structurally the same if and only they are isomorphic. Because of the difficulty of providing a general definition of isomorphism for all possible pairs of set-theoretical entities (models), the standard practice is to provide definitions for each kind of set-theoretical entity. Set-theoretical entities are ordered n-tuples. Isomorphism is defined in terms of the properties of a function such that the domain of the function is the set of entities of the first model, and the range of the function is the set of entities of the second model; the function is a one-to-one function (that is, it effects a one-to-one mapping from one model to the other); and any members of A satisfy any operation in the first model if and only if the corresponding members under the function satisfy the operation which occupies the same position in the n-tuple definition of the other model.

In brief, a theory is formalized by defining a set-theoretical predicate. A model of the theory is an entity which satisfies the set-theoretical predicate. Suppes provides the following example of a mathematical theory formalized by defining a set-theoretical predicate (in appendix A to this chapter I set out Suppes' set-theoretical predicate for classical particle mechanics):

T1:   An algebra $<A,o>$ is a group if and only if for every x, y, and z in A

A1. $x \, o \, (y \, o \, z) \, o \, z$;

A2.   there is a w in A such that

$$x = y \, o \, w$$

A3.   there is a w in A such that

$$x = w \, o \, y$$

A1–A3 are the axioms of the theory.

There are a number of advantages to formalizing theories by defining a set-theoretical predicate rather than by formalizing them in mathematical logic. First, and this point has been alluded to earlier, formalizations in mathematical logic presuppose set-theory along with the results of many other mathematical theories. Moreover, axiomatizations in mathematical logic of theories which use the theorems of theories other than mathematical logic are complex and unnatural, and hence such axiomatizations are extremely difficult, if not impossible, to actually achieve. In effect, one would need to *simultaneously* axiomatize the particular scientific theory, set theory, number theory, and whatever other mathematical and nonmathematical theories will be used in the context of the scientific theory being formalized. And although this is in principle possible, it is in practice an extremely complex and arduous task whose outcome, should someone persevere long enough to achieve it, would be of relatively little value to the actual use and understanding of scientific theories. A set-theoretical approach is a simpler and more natural method of formalization in large part because the full power of set theory can be employed. In addition, it achieves the same level of clarity and precision as axiomatization in mathematical logic.

Second, the comparison of various models for a theory is necessarily *metamathematical* in statement and proof when theories are axiomatized in mathematical logic, but are mathematical when axiomatized by defining a set-theoretical predicate. The comparison of models of theories formalized in mathematical logic requires swapping from the axiomatized theory to a metamathematical framework which includes set theory and then back to the formalized theory. Formalization by defining a set-theoretical predicate enables a direct mathematical statement or proof to be given (see Suppes 1957, pp. 254–255, for an example of such a hybrid proof requiring a metamathematical framework). And since for the purpose of using and understanding scientific theories a comparison of models is fundamental, the set-theoretical approach is less complex, and from a formal point of view, more direct and satisfying. Hence, van Fraassen claims that the slogan Suppes brings to the philosophy of science is that the philosophy of science should be mathematical, and not metamathematical (see van Fraassen 1972, p. 309, and 1980, p. 65).

Third, models of a theory T axiomatized by defining a set-theoretical predicate are exactly the same as models of T axiomatized in mathematical logic.

Fourth, when a theory is formalized by defining a set-theoretical predicate, the empirical application of the theory is separate from the theory. In other words, the task of establishing that the theory actually represents an empirical system involves establishing that an empirical model satisfies the set-theoretical predicate. Establishing this usually involves demonstrating that the empirical model is isomorphic to some model satisfying the predicate. What, in effect, happens is that an empirical system is demonstrated to be structurally and behaviorally equivalent to a model of the predicate, since a model of the predicate will be a system whose structure and behavior are those defined by the predicate.

What this method makes clear is that empirical systems are too complex and "messy" and that the data obtained from investigating them are never in a form that would allow a straightforward comparison with the theory. One needs to employ numerous other theories to demonstrate that an actual empirical system is a system (model) of the kind defined by the predicate. For example, theories of experimental design will be employed to establish that the idealized conditions of an experiment will not lead to a distortion of the empirical system under study. In addition, theories of data analysis will be employed to interpret the raw data obtained from an investigation. Numerous other theories will also be employed. This feature is explored more fully in chapter 6, section 6.1.

What emerges is the complex and extratheoretic character of relating a theory to empirical systems. It is for this reason that the task of relating a theory to the world becomes one of demonstrating that an empirical system is structurally and behaviorally equivalent to a system (a model) which satisfies the set-theoretical predicate. The clearest statement of this aspect of the semantic conception has been given by Ronald Giere (Giere 1979).

4.4. The State Space Approach

Bas van Fraassen and Frederick Suppe have independently developed a semantic conception of the structure of scientific theories that differs in a number of respects from the semantic conception of Suppes. These differences have to do with the way in which the class of models of a theory is defined. They are similar in a large number of ways, including the fact that they represent theories in a way that keeps separate a theory and its method of application. Although there are significant differences between the state space approaches of Suppe and of van Fraassen, I ignore them in this section and set out the general state space approach in the way van Fraassen has developed it. For the purpose of a general exposition, the differences between the views are not important. In subsequent sections, I note only the differences between their accounts which are significant in the context of the point being discussed.

With regard to the general framework, van Fraassen follows Suppes in regarding the formalization of a theory as a definition of the class of models of the theory. All empirical assertions take the form of statements to the effect that a particular empirical system is a kind defined by theory. As with Suppes' set-theoretical predicate approach, van Fraassen's state space approach can be connected to the syntactic conception. Van Fraassen accepts that in principle a theory could be formalized as an axiomatic-deductive structure. In fact, as indicated above, the class of models of the theory can be defined as the structures that satisfy the theorems of an axiomatic and deductive formalization. What van Fraassen does deny, however, is the appropriateness of the axiomatic and deductive formalization. He, quite correctly, holds that it is an impoverished, inaccurate characterization of scientific theories and scientific theorizing.

Both Suppes and van Fraassen consider it the essential job of a scientific theory "to provide us with a family of models, to be used for the representation of empirical phenomena" (van Fraassen 1972, p. 310). Hence, defining the class of models metamathematically as the structures that satisfy the theorems of an axiomatic and deductive structure is unnecessary with regard to the job of the theory. In addition, it is unecessary from a formal point of view, since the class of models can be defined directly without reference to syntactically defined theorems.

Van Fraassen considers his work on the structure of physical theories to be an extension of Beth's semantic analysis of physical theories. His extension involves the provision of a framework, in terms of his own theory of semiinterpreted languages (van Fraassen 1967 and 1969), for Beth's "semantic analysis. In van Fraassen's opinion, Beth's "semantic analysis represents a much more deep-going analysis of the structure of physical theories that the axiomatic and syntactic analysis which depicts such a theory as a symbolic calculus interpreted (partially) by a set of correspondence rules" (van Fraassen 1970, p. 325). He also thinks that Beth's characterization is "more faithful to current practices in foundational research in the sciences than the familiar picture of a partly interpreted axiomatic theory" (van Fraassen, 1970, p. 325).

In general, his approach involves a formalization of theories in terms of meaning relations among predicates. Meaning relations among predicates are represented in a way analogous to the representation of relations of extension by means of Venn diagrams. Venn diagrams involve the choice of a set S and function f which assigns a part of S to each predicate F.

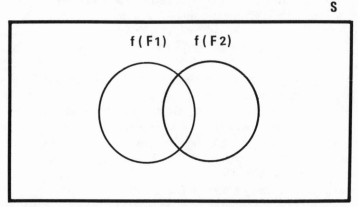

Similarly, relations of intent can be characterized in terms of a logical space T and a mapping function g that maps each predicate F into T (that is, assigns a part of T to each predicate F). A favorite example of van Fraassen's is the case where a function f maps the predicate *is red* into a line segment by assigning a part of the line segment to the predicate. The line segment in this case is the logical space of the color spectrum. Similarly, the predicate *is scarlet* is mapped, by g, into the line segment. The representation of these predicates in the logical space will be as follows:

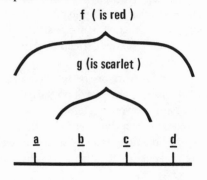

where the points *b* to *c* represent the predicate *is scarlet* and the points *a* to *d* represent the predicate *is red*. In this case the predicate *is scarlet* is intensively included in the predicate *is red*. On the other hand, the predicates *is green* and *is red* intensively exclude each other. The specification of the logical space of a language and an interpretation function provides a semi-interpretation for an uninterpreted artificial language. Hence, the construction of a semi-interpreted language in which relations of intent can be represented will specify three things (van Fraassen 1967, p. 173):

1. The syntax of the language: its vocabulary and grammar

2. The logical space of the language—a set—and an interpretation function

3. The models of the language

It is van Fraassen's contention that

> in natural and scientific language, there are meaning relations among terms which are not merely relations of extension. When a particular part of natural language is adapted for a technical role in the language of science, it is because its meaning structure is especially suitable for this role. And this meaning structure has a representation in terms of a model (always a mathematical structure, and most usually some mathematical space). This language game then has a natural formal reconstruction as an artificial langage the semantics of which is given with reference to this mathematical structure (called a semi-interpreted language . . .,(van Fraassen 1970, p. 327)

In other words, for van Fraassen, theories involve the specification of semi-interpreted languages; consequently, exploring the structure of a semi-interpreted language is one way of exploring what a theory says about the world. The formalization of a physical theory in terms of a semi-interpreted language requires the specification of the following (van Fraassen 1970, pp. 328–329; see also 1972, pp. 311–312).

1. A state space (i.e., logical space) for the physical system defined by the theory

2. A set of measurable physical magnitudes and a set of elementary statements about the system such that each statement assigns a value to a measurable physical magnitude at a particular time

3. A satisfaction function which connects the state space with the elementary statements by assigning a region of the state space to the elementary statement

The specification of a state space involves the specification of a certain topological structure. For example, the state space for classical particles can be taken as a Cartesian six-space,[3] the points of which represent the position and momentum of the particles. The set of measurable physical magnitudes characterizes the physical system and can be represented by reference to the state space. A statement assigning a value to a measurable physical magnitude (i.e., an elementary statement) is mapped into the state space by a satisfaction function such that the mapping determines the set of states in the state space that satisfy the statement. For example, if an elementary statement U assigns a value r to the Y-component of position for a classical particle, the set of states of the system defined by U would be the points of a Cartesian five-space, which is a subset of the Cartesian six-space where the points of this latter space represent the state space of the theory.

For a theory so conceived, as for semi-interpreted languages in general, we can provide definitions of truth, validity, and semantic entailment. If X is a system of the kind defined by the theory and there is a function 'loc' that assigns a location in the state space T to X, then a model for the theory is the couple $< loc, X>$: that is, a model for the theory involves the assignment of the location in the state space of the theory to a system of the kind defined by a theory. Using this characterization of model, truth can be defined as follows.

> An elementary statement U is true in a model M if and only if the location in the state space assigned to X by the 'loc' function belongs to the set of states defined by the satisfaction function, which maps the elementary statement into the state space.

Validity and semantic entailment are defined as follows.

> An elementary statement is a valid sentence in a theory if and only if it is true in every model of the theory.

> A set Y, which is a subset of the set of elementary statements, semantically entails an elementary statement U if and only if U is true in every model of the theory in which every member of Y is true.

For van Fraassen, the language of a theory is a semi-interpreted language. The logic of a theory, though determined by the particular theory is imposed on the semi-interpreted language. Both are incorporated in the topological structure of the state space of the theory.[4]

I conclude this exposition of van Fraassen's state space approach with a summary. Van Fraassen contends that, since certain parts of natural language are adapted for a technical role in the language of science because their meaning structure is especially suited to the role, relations of intent are an important part of the formal structure of physical theories.

The meaning structure has a formal reconstruction as a semi-interpreted artificial language. The construction of a semi-interpreted language involves the specification of a state space, some measureable physical magnitudes, and a satisfaction function that defines the sets of states, in the state space, that satisfy elementary statements which assign a value to measurable physical magnitudes. This semi-interpreted language is the language of the theory, and its meaning structure is given with reference to the state space.

Consequently, for van Fraassen, a theory defines the kinds of systems to which it applies. The definition involves the specification of a state space, the set of all the possible states of the kinds of systems; a family of physical magnitudes; and a satisifaction function which determines a set of states which satisfy the assignment of a value to a physical magnitude (i.e., which determines a set of states in the state space for each value of a physical magnitude).

Physical laws, in this analysis, serve to select the physically possible set of states in the state space (these are laws of coexistence), to select the physically possible trajectories in the state space (these are laws of succession), or to select the physically possible results of interactions of the systems defined by the theory with other systems (these are laws of interaction).[5]

4.5. Summary

According to a recently developed alternative to the syntactic conception, which has become known as the semantic conception of theory structure, a theory is an extralinguistic mathematical entity which consists in the specification—in mathematical English—of a physical system (see Beatty 1980, 1981; Lloyd 1984; Sneed 1971; Stegmuller 1976; Suppe 1972b, 1976, 1977; Suppes 1957, 1967; Thompson 1983b, 1985, 1986, 1987; van Fraassen 1970, 1972, 1980). Theories, understood in this way, define a class of models. Although there are substantive differences between the ways in which the semantics of theories is provided in the syntactic and semantic conceptions, the class of models, defined in a semantic conception, for a theory T is the same as the potential class of models for the formal system of T were it to be formalized in mathematical logic (i.e., formalized in a syntactic conception). Two prominent accounts of the way in which a theory defines a class of models are the set-theoretical account of Patrick Suppes and the state space approach of Bas van Fraassen and Frederick Suppe.

In the semantic conception laws do not describe the behavior of phenomena but specify the behavior of a system. The relationship of a theory to the empirical (phenomenal) system within its intended scope is one of isomorphism: that is, the behavior of a particular phenomenal system is claimed to be isomorphic to the physical system specified by the theory. Establishing this isomorphism is an extratheoretical task. The theory does not specify either the domain of its application or the methodology involved in establishing an isomorphism.

The important features of this conception are as follows (1) theories are semantic structures which specify the behavior of systems, not the behavior of phenomena; (2) phenomena are not explained by deducing them from laws but by asserting that the phenomenal system of which they are a part is isomorphic to the physical system specified by the theory and hence has the same causal structure; (3) the existence and nature of an isomorphic relationship asserted to obtain between a physical system and a phenomenal system are not specified by the theory, and their establishment is complex, requiring reference to theories of experimental design, goodness of fit, analysis and standardization of data, and so forth and to causal chains based on other theories.

Notes

1. Giere (Giere 1979) asserted that theories as definitions have no empirical *content*. His reason for asserting this view is expressed in a later work as follows: "[he has] generally used the term 'theory' [to] refer to a generalized definition or model—which has no empirical content" (Giere 1983, p. 297). However, in this same paper he indicates that in reponse to resistance from scientists and science students, he has decided to compromise on this point in the interest of communication. He asserts that, despite this compromise, "the underlying view of the scientific enterprise, however, is the same" (Giere 1983, p. 298). By "content" I take Giere to mean "empirical applicability" and not "meaning." Hence, it is quite consistent to claim of a particular theory that it has empirical meaning but has no empirical content (no empirical application). Definitions (in the sense used in discussions of scientific theories) do have meaning. It is precisely because proffered definitions have meaning that we can reject some of them as not defining things as they actually are and therefore as not empirically acceptable or applicable (see Thompson 1987 for an example using Euclidean geometry).

2. Suppe has made the point that since theories admit of a number of alternative linguistic formulations ("E.g., classical particle mechanics sometimes is given a Lagrangian formulation and other times is given a Hamiltonian formulation; but it is the same theory regardless which formulation is employed" [Suppe 1972a, p. 130], scientific theories cannot be identified with their linguistic formulations.

3. Although van Fraassen has in various places called classical phase space "Euclidean," he now believes that "Cartesian" is more correct "because Euclidean

now often carries implications about the metric that don't hold there [in classical phase space] (personal communication, 1981).

4. Suppe (Suppe 1977, p. 229) has pointed out that theories so construed impose restrictions both on the sorts of languages used to formulate the theory and on the ways in which phenomena can be described. Suppe considers these features an advantage in that the problem of providing a physical interpretation of quantum mechanics is, in effect, the problem of determining the appropriate logic for quantum mechanics. Consequently, this conception is far more compatible with foundational work in quantum mechanics that is the syntactic conception.

5. For an excellent discussion of the role of laws and meaning postulates in van Fraassen's view, see Wessels 1976.

Appendix A

By way of example, Suppes (1957, p. 294) offers the following set-theoretical predicate formalization of classical particle mechanics:

T2: *A system* $\beta = <P, T, s, m, f, g,>$ *is a system of particle mechanics if and only if the following seven axioms are satisfied:*

Kinematical Axioms

AXIOM P1. *The set P is finite and non-empty.*

AXIOM P2. *The set T is an interval of real numbers.*

AXIOM P3. *For p in P, S_p is twice differentiable on T.*

Dynamical Axioms

AXIOM P4. *For p in P, m(p) is a positive real number.*

AXIOM P5. *For p and q in P and t in T,*

$$f(p, q, t) = -f(q, p, t).$$

AXIOM P6. *For p and q in P and t in T,*

$$s(p, t) \times f(p, q, t) = -s(q, t) \times f(q, p, t).$$

AXIOM P7. *For p in P and t in T,*

$$m(p)D^2 Sp(t) = \sum_{q \in P} f(p, q, t) + g(p, t).$$

CHAPTER 5

A Semantic Conception of the
Structure of Evolutionary Theory

As indicated in previous chapters, an adequate account of an evolutionary theoretical framework must make possible the interaction of several theories, among which are population genetic theory and selection theory. In section 5.1, I provide a semantic conception formalization of population genetic theory. In this way I hope to illustrate the nature of the formalization of the component theories of an evolutionary theoretical framework. In order to illustrate the differences between the set-theoretical approach and the state space approach, I provide simple accounts of both. A much richer and more exhaustive treatment of population genetic theory in the state space approach can be found in Lloyd 1983 and in press. In section 5.2, I discuss one important way in which the semantic conception of population genetic theory is more faithful to foundational work in genetics. This, in addition to the other advantages set out in this book, is a significant advantage. In other words, in addition to providing a richer and more heuristically valuable account of the logic of the relation between a theory and the world, the semantic conception more accurately describes the actual practice of biologists involved in foundational work. In section 5.3, I discuss the structure of evolutionary theory as a family of interacting models in the state space approach.

5.1. A Semantic Conception of Population Genetics

One important theoretical component of the evolutioanry theoretical framework, called the modern synthetic theory of evolution, is population genetic theory. The extent of its importance can be seen in the fact that phenotypic changes in a population, insofar as they are interesting from an evolutionary point of view, must be related to changes in the genotypes of the population. Unfortunately, this fact has caused some biologists and philosophers (see chapter 3) mistakenly (for the reasons given in chapters 1 and 3) to *define* evolution in genetical terms. Dobzhansky, for example, claims that "evolution is a change in the genetic composition of populations" (Dobzhansky 1951, p.

16). Indeed, influenced by Dobzhansky (for whose work I have in all other respects the greatest admiration and from whom I have learned a great many sophisticated aspects of genetic theory) and by Ruse, I argued, in a previous paper (Thompson 1983b), that population genetics was the dynamical core of evolutionary theory because evolutionary changes were in effect changes in genotype frequencies. As can be easily gathered from the preceding chapters, I now think that this view is seriously in error.

What I undertake in this section, then, is a semantic conception formalization of population genetic theory in both a set-theoretical approach and a state space approach. A semantic conception formalization of the modern synthetic theory of evolution requires the separate formalization of other theories and the development of a framework within which these theories interact.

The genetics of populations is extremely complex. For instance, there are a large number of loci and a multiple number of alternative alleles for each locus. Hence, there are a large number of possible pairs of alleles for each locus. In addition, pairs of alleles at one locus can, and frequently do, interact with pairs of alleles at one or more other loci. These features produce a level of complexity which is difficult to handle. Hence, some simplification is necessary in order to make possible an exposition. Typically, the simplification takes the form of restricting one's attention to single loci with at most three alternative alleles. This is the strategy I adopt in this chapter.

The physical systems to which population genetic theory applies are groups of conspecific interbreeding individuals. These groups are called "demes," "genetic populations," or, for convenience, simply "populations." From a genetic point of view, a population is a set of genotypes where a genotype is a pair of alleles at a particular locus.[1] Change in a population, from one generation to the next, is a function of the relative frequency of genotypes in each generation. In other words, a change in the relative number of genotypes from one generation to the next constitutes a genetic change in that population from one generation to the next. Changes in the relative frequency of genotypes results from one or more of the following; the shuffling and recombination of alleles during meiosis and gamete union; the addition of alleles by mutation or immigration; the deletion of alleles by mutation, emigration or selective pressure; or, in the case of small populations, sampling error. Simple Mendelian genetics (i.e., genetics based only on Mendel's two laws) deals with the shuffling and recombination of alleles during meiosis. The more sophisticated current population genetic theory also deals with the other causes of change. However, as already argued, many of these other causes of change are the result of processes described by other theories and therefore are not appropriately described by a *genetic* theory. What population genetic theory ought to do is to describe the effect of these factors on the population—genetical system: that is, these factors are inputs to the population-genetical system which cause change within it but which are the causal product of another system.

John Beatty (Beatty 1981) has provided the bare bones of a set-theoretical predicate approach to the structure of population genetics. Beatty states:

> On the semantic view, a theory is not comprised of laws of nature. Rather, a theory is just the specification of a kind of system—more a definition than an empirical claim. In the case of the synthetic theory, an appropriate system specification is:
>
> A Mendelian breeding group = [df] a breeding group whose members form gametes in accordance with Mendel's first law of inheritance.
>
> Since the Hardy-Weinberg law is a deductive consequence of Mendel's first law, we can also say of a Mendelian Breeding group that:
>
> A Mendelian breeding group = [by consequence of its df] a breeding group whose genetic frequencies obey the Hardy-Weinberg law. (Beatty 1981, p. 410)

What Beatty means when he denies that theories, in a semantic conception, are "not comprised of laws of nature" is that laws, in a semantic conception, do not describe the behavior of phenomena (they do not state *empirical regularities*)—they describe the behavior of systems (they *define*, in part, the behavior of a system). Moreover, theories are not *comprised* of laws in a semantic conception, but contain laws as part of the definition of the system. In a syntactic conception, theories *are* deductively related laws (interpreted theorems).

In presenting Beatty's account, I stated that he gives the bare bones of a set-theoretical approach to the structure of population genetic theory—which was all he required for his purposes. As is clear from what he says, he takes himself to be giving an account of the "synthetic theory." What he in effect offers is an account of a Mendelian breeding group, as is obvious from the definiendum of the definition. Beatty, when this paper was written, held a view similar to that of Ruse (a view I also held at that time), according to which population genetics was the core (or identical with) the synthetic theory. Hence, it was quite natural for him to link an account of population genetic theory with the synthetic theory in the way he did. One thing that emerges from Beatty's paper is that even if Ruse is correct about evolutionary theory, the semantic view is a richer and more logically accurate account of the core theory. In addition, Beatty's argument is unaffected by this identification. With minor modifications, his argument remains very compelling, even for the account of the modern synthetic theory given in this book.

What Beatty has provided is not a formal characterization of a set-theoretical predicate but rather a statement of the essential thrust of such a predicate and of its ultimate character as a definition of a system. A formal presentation is as follows:

T: A system $\beta = <P, A, f, g>$ is a Mendelian breeding system if and only if the following axioms are satisfied:

Axiom 1. The sets P and A are finite and nonempty.

Axiom 2. For any $a \in P$ and $l, m \in A$,

$$f(a, l) \ \& \ f(a, m) \text{ iff } l = m.$$

Axiom 3. For any $a, b, \in P$ and $l \in A$,
$$g(a, l) \ \& \ g(b, l) \text{ iff } a = b.$$

Axiom 4. For any $a, b \in P$ and $l \in L$ such that $f(a, l)$ and $f(b, l)$, $g(a, l)$ is independent of $g(b, l)$.

Axiom 5. For any $a, b \in P$ and $l, m \in L$ such that $f(a, l)$ and $f(b, m)$, $g(a, l)$ is independent of $g(b, m)$.

Where P and A are sets and f and g are functions. P is the set of all alleles in the populations, A is the set of all loci in the population. If $a \in P$ and $l \in A$, then $f(a, l)$ is an assignment, in a diploid phase of a cell, of a to l (i.e., f is a function that assigns a as an alternative allele at locus l). If $a \in P$, and $l \in A$, then $g(a, l)$ is the gamete formed, by meiosis, with a being at l in the gamete (the haploid phase of the cell).

Although more sophistication could be introduced into this example, the example as it stands illustrates adequately the nature of a set-theoretical approach to the formalization of population genetic theory in its simple Mendelian system form. More axioms and more functions would need to be added to adequately define a system in which other important aspects, such as meiotic drive or selection, were taken into account. As indicated above, however, in a number of cases the factors which will affect a population-genetical system are the result of another system and not a population-genetical system. For example, selection will be an input to a population-genetical system, the input being the outcome of the behavior of a defined phenotypic selection system. Linkage and crossing over will also be inputs from chromosomal theory. Hence, a number of the additional axioms of a more sophisticated account will specify how the system behaves under inputs.

I turn now to the state space approach. Since population genetic theory is a theory about the change, from one generation to the next, of the relative frequency of genotypes in a population, any formal account of the theory, in a semantic conception, will involve the specification of the physically possible states of populations in terms of genotype frequencies as well as the physically possible changes, under isolation and interaction, of genotype frequencies.

In order to simplify the formalization, I begin by assuming that populations are isolated systems in the sense that no mutations, migrations, or environmental changes (i.e., changes in selective pressures) take place. Towards the end of the discussion I indicate how migration, selective pressure, and so forth are taken into account when populations are not assumed to be isolated. In addition, I shall assume that populations are large, thus eliminating the importance of gamete sampling error; that the individuals in a population mate randomly in that no phenotypic expression of the genotypes is involved in mate selection; and that genotype frequencies are the same for both sexes. These are common simplifying assumptions of population genetic theory.

The pure part of population genetic theory, in the van Fraassen state space approach, will define the kind of system to which the theory applies. The first step in defining the kind of physical system to which the theory applies is the specification of the set of states of which the system is capable. The formal specification of this set of states involves the specification of "a collection of mathematical entities (numbers, vectors, functions) to be used to represent these states" (van Fraassen 1972, p. 311). This collection is the state space of this kind of system. In the case of population genetic theory, the state space will be a Cartesian n-space where 'n' is a function of the number of possible pairs of alleles in the population. A law of coexistence to the effect that only alleles at the same locus can form pairs will select the class of physically possible pairs of alleles. States of the system (genotype frequencies of populations) are n-tuples of real numbers from zero to one and are represented in the state space as points.

The second thing the theory specifies is a set of measurable physical magnitudes. These magnitudes are represented with reference to the state space (i.e., they are represented by a function defined on the state space). In the case of population genetic theory, they are genotype frequencies represented by real numbers greater than or equal to zero and less than or equal to one. Statements which formulate propositions to the effect that a particular magnitude has a particular value at a particular time are elementary statements. For example, the statement that a genotype Aa at a polymorphic locus has a frequency of 0.5 in the population is an elementary statement.

Finally, a theory must specify a satisfaction function for every elementary statement such that for each elementary statement U the satisfaction function h specifies a set of states in the state space that satisfy U. For example, the satisfaction function for the statement "genotype Aa occurs with a frequency of 0.5″ would specify the set of states in the state space that satisfy the statement. In this case the set of states would be a Cartesian $(n\text{-}1)$-space, which is a subset of the state space.

The set of elementary statements interpreted in terms of the state space is an elementary language. It is worth noting that van Fraassen wants it to be clear that "an elementary language associated with a given theory is by no means a language in which the theory can be formulated. It is a language in which statments about the subject matter of the theory can be formulated. Exploring the structure of the elementary language is one way of exploring what the theory says about the world" (van Fraassen 1972, p. 312). It is, in other words, the language of the theory.

Laws of succession specify the possible histories of the members of the kind of physical system defined by the theory. In the case of population genetic theory, a central law of succession is the Hardy-Weinberg law.[2] This law specifies the possible histories of a population by specifying the genotype frequencies of one generation at a particular locus (a subspace of the state space) on the basis of the genotype frequencies of the previous generation at that locus. As an illustration, consider the case of a single autosomal locus at which combinations of two possible alleles, A and a, occur. Suppose that the genotypes AA, Aa, and aa are present with a frequency f_1, f_2 and f_3 respectively, in the population. Suppose also that the fitness (a transformation function—see below) of each genotype is 1 (i.e., they are equally and maximally fit). On the basis of the above frequencies, the proportion of alleles at the locus can be calculated. If p represents the proportion of A alleles, and q represents the proportion of a alleles, then

$$p = (2f_1 + f_2)/2, \text{ and}$$

$$q = (f_2 + 2f_3)/2.$$

The Hardy-Weinberg law specifies that a population with p proportion of A alleles and q proportion of a alleles in generation 1 where A and a are the only possible alleles at a locus will give rise to the following genotype frequencies in generation 2:

$$p^2(AA) : 2pq(Aa) : q^2(aa).$$

Where the fitness value for one or more of the genotypes is not 1, the case is more complex but still employs the Hardy-Weinberg law. What changes is the proportion $p : q$ of the alleles. Consider, for example, a case similar to the above except that the fitness values of AA, Aa, and aa are 1, 1, and 0.5, respectively. If the frequencies of the genotypes before selection in generation 1 are

$$f_1(Aa) : f_2(Aa) : f_3(aa),$$

then the frequencies after selection will be

$$(f_1(1)/W) \, AA : (f_2(1)/W) \, Aa : f(f_3(0.5)/W) \, aa,$$

where $W = f_1(1) + f_2(1) + f_3(0.5)$. This is an instance of the transformation function (in effect, another law of succession):

$$g(fx) = (f_x)(s_x)/(f_i)(s_i),$$

where $(f_i)(s_i)$ is the sum of the initial frequency times the fitness of each genotype for all possible genotypes at a locus, (f_x) is the initial frequency of genotype x at that locus, and (s_x) *is the fitness of genotype* x at that locus.

Thus, the proportions of alleles in generation 1 will be

$$p = (2f_1 + f_2)/2W$$

$$q = (f_2 + 2f_3(0.5)/2W.$$

To determine the genotype frequencies in generation 2, the values of p and q are substituted for p and q in the Hardy-Weinberg law (i.e., $p^2 \, Aa : 2pq \, Aa : q^2 \, aa$). In a similar way, the application of the law is more involved but no less valid in cases of more polymorphic loci as over against loci with only two alleles, and is unaffected by assuming that the system is not isolated. Other laws of succession will take account of meiotic drive and so forth.

So far I have assumed that the systems defined by the theory are isolated except for the inclusion of selective pressure. This, however, is not the case with actual populations—mutations, migrations, and so forth do occur. Hence, population genetic theory, since it defines the systems to which it applies, cannot be such that it defines only isolated systems. Populations must be understood as systems with input. The inputs are of two kinds, addition or deletion of alleles and changes of genotype fitness. In the case of changes of genotype fitness, the change results from changes in the environment of the population. As such it involves the interaction of two systems. Similarly, the addition or deletion of alleles due to migration involves the interaction of a population with other populations (i.e., systems). The case of mutation is less clear, though it is reasonable and convenient to assume that mutation involves the interaction of a population with another system (i.e., some outside factors)—perhaps biochemical.

In the case of systems with input, the theory will, through laws of interaction, specify the possible outcomes of the interactions of the system with other systems. These laws of interaction require the specification of a nonempty set of states S (i.e., the state space of the system), a nonempty set of inputs I, and a "next state" function that maps $S \times I$ into S. Hence, laws of interaction will take the form

$$(S_k, i_1i_2) = S_{k+1},$$

where S_k and S_{k+1} are successive states of the system and i_1i_2 (written without commas) are inputs (see Ginsburg 1960). As van Fraassen has noted, the most satisfying way to deal with interacting systems is to view them as a single large system. This, he notes, is not always possible, becaues often the systems are quite dissimilar (van Fraassen 1970, p. 332). This is indeed the case with regard to populations and environments. It is not, however, the case with regard to migration in and out of populations. In this case the systems of interactions are very similar. The reasons for not viewing these systems as a single larger system are the desire for simplicity and manageability, and the desire to conform to actual biological practice.

5.2. Faithfulness to Foundational Work in Genetics

What advantage do these semantic conception accounts of population genetic theory have over the syntactic conception account of Ruse? One significant advantage is that they quite naturally correspond to the ways in which biologists expound, employ, and explore the theory. The semantic conception considers a theory to be a definition of a system which is, in part, a description of the behavior of the system it defines. The systems are highly abstract and relate to phenomena through a complex hierarchy of other theories. Consequently, in a semantic conception the relationship of the theory to phenomena is not specified by the theory, whereas in a syntactic conception it is specified through correspondence rules.

This distinction between the theory as a definition of a system and the relating of the system defined by the theory to phenomena within its intended scope of application corresponds quite naturally to the way biologists expound, employ, and explore population genetic theory. Consider, for example, Lewontin's discussions of population genetic theory (Lewontin 1974 and 1980). First, Lewontin has expressed views about theories that are clearly more faithfully represented by a semantic account. For example, he claims that "theory generally should not be an attempt to say how the world is.

Rather, it is an attempt to construct the logical relations that arise from various assumptions about the world. It is an 'as if' set of conditional statements" (Lewontin 1980, p. 65) On the specific character of evolutionary theory, he claims, "The problem of constructing an evolutionary theory is the problem of constructing a state space that will be dynamically sufficient, and a set of transformations in that state space that will transform all the state-variables" (Lewontin 1974, p. 8). This is precisely how theories are construed in a semantic conception.

Second, Lewontin's account of the biological controversies surrounding aspects of the genetic basis of evolutionary change provides clear evidence that actual biological practice is more faithfully accounted for by the semantic conception. The controversy concerning classical and balance theories of population structure is a case in point.

The classical theory asserts that all individuals in a population are homozygous for "wild-type" alleles at almost every locus. In addition, at a very small number of loci each individual is heterozygous for some rare deleterious alleles. In this view, two randomly selected individuals from the population would have genetic descriptions as follows:

where ' + ' represents wild-type alleles and 'm' represents a deleterious mutant.

The balance theory asserts that all individuals in a population are heterozygous at almost every locus. In this view, two randomly selected individuals from the population would have genetic descriptions as follows:

A	B
$A_4 B_3 C_7 D_6 E_1 \ldots Z_3$	$A_1 B_8 C_2 D_3 E_7 \ldots Z_6$
-----------------------	-----------------------
-----------------------	-----------------------
$A_2 B_1 C_5 D_2 E_1 \ldots Z_5$	$A_3 B_4 C_2 D_1 E_3 \ldots Z_5$

The number of alleles at each locus is assumed to be exceptionally large.

Without this assumption the population would, in accordance with Mendel's laws, become homozygous.

A comparison of the consequences that follow from each theory reveals three essential differences. First, the classical theory entails that most genetic diversity within a polymorphic species is interpopulational. Thus, differences between populations of polymorphic species are extremely important from an evolutionary point of view. The balance view, on the other hand, entails that a large amount of genetic diversity exists within a population. Hence, interpopulational differences are of less evolutionary consequence. Second, the classical theory assumes that the main role of natural selection is the removal of deleterious mutant alleles from the population. The balance theory, on the other hand, assumes some form of balancing selection, such as heterozygote superiority. The case of sickle-cell anaemia is an example of this balancing selection. The heterozygote is superior in fitness to either homozygote because it does not develop sickle-cell anaemia (as does the ss homozygote) nor does it contract malaria (as does the NN homozygote). Third, the classical theory assumes that speciation is dependent on the occurrence of advantageous mutations because populations are almost entirely homozygous. The balance theory, on the other hand, assumes that there is always a large amount of genetic variation to serve as a basis for speciation.

What is interesting about these competing theories is the logical way that biologists view them. Lewontin claims that they are not perceived as alternative interpretations of ambiguous observations but "as *a priori* predictions about what would be observed if a method could actually be found to describe the distribution of genotypes in a population" (Lewontin 1974, p. 28). Lewontin understands them to be alternative descriptions of kinds of physical systems and holds that all empirical claims concerning them involve assertions that certain empirical systems (e.g., populations) are physical systems of the kind described by the theory. Even Ruse concedes that this is the way biologists view these genetical theories. In his discussion of the biological debate over the classical theory and the balance theory, he concludes: "Hence, in actual practice the debate between population geneticists seems to be about which models actually apply in nature" (Ruse 1977a, p. 102).

What emerges from this discussion is that the semantic conception of the structure of scientific theories is, as van Fraassen has claimed, "more faithful to current practice in foundational research in the science, than the familiar picture of a partly interpreted axiomatic theory" (van Fraassen 1970, p. 325). It certainly appears to be more faithful to foundational research in population genetics.

This is one significant advantage of the semantic conception. In what follows in the next section and in chapters 5 and 6, I shall argue that there are a considerable number of other advantages to adopting a semantic conception.

5.3. A Semantic Conception of Evolutionary Theory as a Family of Interacting Models

In chapter 1, I argued that an adequate evolutionary theoretical framework was a family of interacting theories and not a unified theory. In chapter 3, I argued that the syntactic accounts of 'evolutionary theory' given by Ruse and by Williams and Rosenberg are inadequate and that at the root of their inadequacy is the fact that they distort evolutionary theory in order to have a unified theory to axiomatize. Ruse distorts it by identifying it with population genetic theory, and Williams and Rosenberg distort it by identifying it with selection theory. In this chapter, I indicate how an evolutionary theoretical framework understood as a family of interacting theories can be accurately represented in a semantic account.

If one were constrained to formalize 'evolutionary theory' within a syntactic conception, then one would either have to live with one of the distortions mentioned above or accept that 'evolutionary theory' was not capable of being formalized—at least not at present. For some this latter admission is paramount to admitting that it is not a genuine scientific theory or that it is not a scientific theory of the kind Newtonian mechanics is, and that therefore evolutionary biology is a different kind of science.

I do not think that any of these views are entailed by the admission that it cannot be formalized within a syntactic conception. For one thing, even Newtonian mechanics, as already argued, cannot in any natural or simple way be formalized within a syntactic conception. And certainly relativity theory and quantum mechanics cannot be adequately formalized in a syntactic conception. In addition, there are numerous reasons why, even if such a formalization were possible, it is not desirable. These are set out in section 2.6. Consequently, even if one had only the syntactic conception of theory structure with which to work, the fact that evolutionary theory did not fit it would not make evolutionary theory a different kind of theory, nor would attempts to force it, by distortion, into the syntactic conception mould be useful, since the conception is clearly flawed. One does not, however, have only the syntactic conception with which to work. One also has the much richer semantic conception. What the semantic conception offers is a way of formalizing theories of physics and evolutionary theory that does not involve distortion and that avoids the undesirable features of the syntactic conception.

I have argued that fundamental to any formalization of an adequate evolutionary theoretical framework is the need to be able to represent it as a family of interacting theories. In a semantic conception, two theories can interact on at least two levels. First, there can be inputs to a physical system which result from its interaction with another system such that the state of the system is altered. The laws of interaction will specify, by means of a 'next state' function, the possible outcomes which result from these inputs. That is, a 'next state' function maps $S \times I$ into S where S is a nonempty set of states and I is a nonempty set of inputs. In this way one system will directly affect the behavior of another system.

A second level of interaction can, and almost always does, occur when a theory is applied to phenomena. For example, whenever an apparatus is used to make scientific observations, as is almost always the case, there will be an interaction between the theory being applied and a theory or theories which describe the behavior of the apparatus. Suppe (Suppe 1974, pp. 74–79) considers it the job of a theory of experimental design (a part of the theory of the experiment on his taxonomy) to specify the ways in which these theories interact—or, as he expounds it, the ways in which the phenomenal systems to which the two theories apply interact. The laws of interaction in this case will not be part of the theory being applied but part of the theory of the experiment used to apply the theory to a phenomenal system. Without a theory of the experiment containing laws of interaction, it would not be possible to causally explain why the apparatus (usually a phenomenal system within the intended scope of a theory other than the one being applied) is an observation within the phenomenal system to which the theory is being applied—recall Schaffner's criticism of the syntactic conception, outlined above in chapter 2, on exactly this point.[3]

The interaction of the theory of natural selection and population genetic theory, as required by the view that evolutionary theory is best characterized as a family of interacting theories, is of the first level: that is, the theories directly interact with each other. On the one hand, population genetic theory directly interacts with the theory of natural selection. The laws of interaction in this case will specify, by means of a 'next state' function, the phenotypic next state of the population between selections and across generations. In other words, a population will undergo selection in accordance with the laws of succession of the theory of natural selection (S is mapped into S) and then the laws of interaction of the theory will specify the next state of the system (the next generation) by specifying how the system behaves under inputs determined by the theory of heredity ($S \times I$ is mapped into S).

Conversely, the theory of natural selection directly interacts with population genetic theory. The laws of interaction in this case will specify, by means of a 'next state' function, the genotypic next state of the population after selection. In other words, the genotype of the population will undergo generational transition in accordance with the laws of succession of popuation genetic theory, and then the laws of interaction of the theory will specify the next state of the system (the state after selection) by specifying how the system behaves under inputs which are determined by the theory of natural selection or ecology.

In this view, within an evolutionary theoretical framework, each theory is dependent on the other. Without interaction neither theory is an adequate description of evolutionary change. And this is precisely the characterization of 'evolutionary theory' that was argued for in chapters 1 and 3—a characterization that could not be accommodated by the syntactic conception. Consequently, the semantic conception of theories provides a framework within which a formalization of 'evolutionary theory' understood as a family of interacting theories can be given, whereas the syntactic conception does not. The semantic conception is consequently a richer account of theory structure and the more appropriate and promising account within which to formalize evolutionary theory.

The semantic conception, unlike the syntactic conception, accommodates complex explanatory frameworks because theories—which are extralinguistic entities that define a class of models—can interact. Hence, a phenomenon can be explained by choosing from the theories that make up the framework the theory most relevant to the phenomenon, and then using other theories in the framework to determine the values of the required inputs to the principal theory. In this way, other theories can be used in applying a given theory to empirical phenomena even though they are independent of the principal theory. In the case of evolutionary theory, application of any of its component theories to the explanation or prediction of *evolutionary* phenomena requires inputs from a number of other component theories without which the explanation or prediction is not *evolutionary*. In other words, although a quite acceptable explanation of a nonevolutionary genetical phenomenon may well be able to be given in terms of population genetic theory alone, an adequate explanation of an evolutionary phenomenon cannot be given even if the phenomenon is at a genetical level. For example, if the phenomenon to be explained is a change in gene frequency and that change is a function of selection at the level of the phenotype, then population genetic theory alone will be inadequate. What are required are inputs to the population genetic system from the phenotypic selection theory.

Consider, for example, Ruse's account of the evolutionary explanation of Darwin's finches (Ruse 1973, pp. 52–59). Ruse, drawing on work done by Lack (Lack 1947), points out that there is a cluster of phenomena to be explained in the case of Darwin's finches, a subfamily of the finch family which is found on the Galapagos Archipelago. First, there is a fact that the finches on the islands are often similar to the finches on the mainland but differ in important ways from them. Second, on many of the islands there are endemic forms of Darwin's finches, that is, finches that are similar to those on other islands but that differ in important ways. Third, this similarity is found primarily in birds, reptiles, and insects. In general, islands which are some distance from the mainland do not have mammals, and the rare cases where they do the mammals are very different form those on the mainland. These phenomena all have to do with the geographic distribution of organisms.

The principal explanatory concept used by Lack for explaining these phenomena is 'geographical isolation', which entails 'reproductive isolation'. The more isolated islands are from each other and from the mainland by bodies of water which are difficult to traverse, the greater will be the evolutionary divergence of finches on each island from those on other islands and from those on the mainland. Geographic isolation, therefore, explains the differences: populations of finches reproductively isolated from each other evolve in different ways. It also explains the absence of mammals, since the greater the difficulty in traversing the distance between the islands and the mainland, the less likely mammals are to attempt it or to succeed. It also explains the presence of the finches (and other organisms such as reptiles and insects), since finches have some chance of traversing the distance between the mainland and between islands or of being blown off course and ending up on an island different from their home island or their mainland home. This in turn explains the similarity of island finches to each other and to those on the mainland: although infrequent because of the difficulty of successfully traversing the distances and the natural timidity of finches to try the crossing, finches do traverse the distance. Hence, founding populations on an island will have come from the mainland or from another island but these founding populations will subsequently experience an extremely low level of immigration from the mainland and other islands.

Ruse concedes that this explanation is most likely correct. He argues, however, that it is incomplete. What is missing is an explanation of why isolated populations of organisms should evolve into new species. To answer this question, Ruse contends that one must turn to population genetic theory. Population genetic theory can explain why isolated gene pools undergo changes that result in the evolution of new species. Indeed, using population genetics, one can explain why a very small founding population (perhaps even one gravid female) can very rapidly evolve into a new species. The genetics of this phenomenon of rapid speciation is referred to as the "founder effect" (or principle).

Ruse, of course, is correct in pointing out that explaining why isolated populations evolve into new species requires an appeal to population genetic theory. However, his charge of incompleteness against Lack can be leveled at his own account. Although the biogeographic account given by Lack explains the various phenomena, it does so by assuming that isolated populations will evolve into new species. However, although the population-genetical account given by Ruse explains the phenomena, it assumes, among other things, reproductive isolation and selection pressure. The biogeographic account may need to be supplemented by population genetic theory and selection theory, but the genetic account needs to be supplemented by biogeography and selection theory. How, other than by an appeal to biogeographical theorizing, could one adequately explain the phenomenon of isolation, which is required for the population-genetical explanation to be justified? How, other than by an appeal to theorizing about the principles under which selection occurs (which will involve ecological theorizing), could one adequately explain the occurrence of selective pressure (different on each population) on the island populations, which is required for the population-genetical explanation to be justified? Without input from these other domains of theorizing, the population-genetical explanation is as incomplete and speculative as the biogeographic account alone or an ecological account alone. In short, all three (and no doubt more) theoretical domains need to be brought to bear in order for an adequate *evolutionary* explanation to be given.

In this case the relevant principal theory, were it sufficiently well developed, could be biogeography with inputs from population genetic theory and selection theory. It is not, however, in my opinion, well enough developed. Hence, population genetic theory can serve as the principal theory with inputs from selection theory and biogeography. There is no primacy of population genetic theory here, only a practical decision based on the developed state of the theory. All the theories are equally required for an adequate explanation to be given. Which one of them is chosen as primary in a given case is based on numerous considerations, including the domain of theorizing within which the explanation is being developed as well as the sophistication of the various theories relative to the need for sophistication in the particular case.

This example illustrates the central thesis of this chapter: a Darwinian evolutionary framework consists of a number of interacting theories. Therefore, any formal account of the logic of this framework must capture this interactive character. The semantic conception of theory structure is well suited to this task. The syntactic conception is not.

Notes

1. The term *genotype* is also used to refer to the entire genetic structure of an organism. When, as in this chapter, *genotype* is used in the context of discussions of "genotype frequencies," it means pairs of alleles at a particular locus. In most cases the context of its use will determine the meaning of the term. In this chapter it means pairs of alleles at a locus.

2. Suppe (1976) has drawn a distinction between laws of succession and laws of

quasisuccession. Given this distinction, the Hardy-Weinberg law is a law of quasisuccession.

3. For a detailed account of this level of interaction in a semantic conception see Suppe 1974, pp. 74–79.

CHAPTER 6

Sociobiology

In this chapter I argue that some of the controversy surrounding socio-biology can be more clearly understood and resolved by adopting a semantic conception of thoery structure. Indeed, I argue that adherence to the syntactic conception has resulted in a misdescription of the problems with sociobiology and an impoverished understanding of its theoretical character and the ways in which sociobiology can take seriously the cultural determinants of behavior.

6.1. Explanation and Testability

In chapter 1, I pointed out that since the publication of *Sociobiology: The New Synthesis* (Wilson 1975) a number of biologists and philosophers have claimed that the sociobiological enterprise is untestable (and, for some, there-fore unscientific) (see Burian 1978; Gould 1976, 1978; Lewontin 1977). It is untestable, according to the critics, because sociobiological explanations (and, by inference, predictions) are highly speculative and ad hoc. As indi-cated in chapter 1, a central reason for this problem, according to the critics, is that the genetic basis of the phenomena which are being explained or pre-dicted in terms of evolutionary theory is assumed without evidence, and any evidence that might suggest nongenetic transmission (as, for example, the in-credible short time span—in evolutionary and genetic terms—during which cultural change takes place) is rendered impotent by the postulation of ad hoc mechanisms (for example, the multiplier effect). These features, they con-tend, make the sociobiological enterprise immune to evidence (and in some views of science, therefore, unscientific) and sociobiological explanations lit-tle more than fascinating storytelling.

In this section, I argue that although this is a methodological problem for sociobiology, it can in a semantic conception of theories, be clearly identified as a problem with the application of sociobiological theory to phenomena (i.e., behavior, specifically human behavior) and not with the theory itself. Specifically, it is a problem with the causal sequence of theories employed in relating sociobiolgial theory to human behavior. This analysis, I contend, is

101

a more thoroughgoing analysis than that provided by the critics and than is possible in a syntactic conception account of theories. One important outcome of this analysis will be a plausible account of why sociobiological theory is so successfully employed in explaining animal behavior, especially insect behavior—a success freely admitted by some of the critics[1]—and yet so apparently problematic when employed to explain human behavior (and perhaps that of some other higher organisms).

My strategy in explicating the problem involved in applying sociobiological theory to human behavior is two-staged. First, I examine relevant logical and epistemological aspects of the successful application of evolutionary theory to the phenomenon of sickle-cell anaemia—an application which results in a widely accepted explanation of the persistence of this disease. Second, I examine, in light of the discussion of sickle-cell anaemia, a controversial application of sociobiological theory to human behavior, namely, that of explaining the persistence of homosexual behavior in human populations.

Consider the case of a person who manifests impaired growth and development, increased susceptibility to infection, severe abdominal pain with normal bowel sounds and no rebound tenderness, paleness, and physical weakness. These symptoms are explained in certain cases by reference to hemolytic anaemia resulting from the sickling of red blood cells. This explanation appeals to a theory of physiology which describes, among other things, the structure, internal behavior, and function of red blood cells in the body as well as the physiological effects of an abnormal red blood cell structure. The sickling of the red blood cells is explained by reference to the fact that, in the case of those with sickle-cell anaemia, the nucleotide sequence, which determines the structure of the protein hemoglobin, codes for the amino acid valine in the sixth position on the, β-chain instead of glutamic acid, as is normally the case. This substitution, under reduced oxygen tension, results in the valines at positions 6 and 1 forming a hydrophobic association which leads to a conformation that stacks in such a way as to distort the erythrocyte and thus cause the sickle shape. This explanation appeals to molecular biological theory, which describes, among numerous other things, how the nucleotide sequences of DNA determine the structure of proteins, and to biochemical theory, which describes the behavior of biochemical structures. Hence, by an appeal to a number of different theoretical frameworks, a connection between the physical characteristics cited and a sequence of nucleotides is made and the physical characteristics are explained.

Given the character of the physical condition and the high mortality rate associated with it, an explanation of the persistence of this physical condition has been sought. The current explanation of this persistence refers to the increased fitness, in malaria-infested environments, of individuals who are heterozygous for the sickle-cell allele (i.e., have one allele for sickle-cell hemoglobin and one for normal hemoglobin at the same locus). In other words, the heterozygote has slightly increased protection against *Plasmodium falciparum* malaria and hence, in malaria-infested areas, gains a selective advantage over either homozygote— one will suffer from sickle cell anaemia and the other will have less protection against malaria. This explanation involves an application of evolutionary theory to the phenomenon of sickle-cell anaemia. Evolutionary theory describes the laws of succession governing the behavior of alleles, the effects of selection on the genome, the laws of succession under various modes of selection at various levels, and so forth. And it is in terms of the parameters (alleles, popu lations, etc.) and the laws governing the behavior of a physical system described by the theory that the explanation is given.

The application of evolutionary theory to sickle-cell anaemia in this ex- planation is mediated by the causal sequence of theories outlined in the above discussion of the explanation of the physical condition. In other words, the physical condition described above is related to the physiological condition of sickled red blood cells by a theory of physiology. The physiological condition is in turn related to the genotype of the organisms involved by molecular genetical theory and biochemical theory. What in effect this causal sequence of theories does is to causally relate the physical condition to the genotype. This causal relationship is an important feature in the application of evolu- tionary theory to the sickle-cell anaemia case, in the following way.

The behavior of the component system (the population-genetical one) of evolutionary theory that is relevant to this case is the system defined by popu- lation genetic theory. And the behavior of this system is specified by the laws of succession governing the behavior of genotypes under various conditions, including selection, in a state space. In the case of sickle-cell anaemia, among the parameters and laws which determine the behavior of the relevant system are gene loci, alleles, selection coefficients, and the Hardy-Weinberg law of succession. In order to relate the behavior of this system to the behavior of organisms at the phenomenal level, the above outlined causal sequence of theories must be employed to relate the parameters of the physical system (i.e., alleles, etc.) and their behavior to those of the physical conditions of or- ganisms (i.e., pain, bowel sounds, physical weakness, susceptibility to infec- tion, resistance to malaria, etc.) which are, in turn, related to reproductive success.

Consider now the case of homosexual behavior and the sociobiological explanation of its persistence in the population despite the presumed evolu- tionary disadvantage of the behavior; it is assumed that those who engage in homosexual behavior will leave few, if any, offspring and therefore, like those with sickle-cell anaemia, are less fit, from an evolutionary point of view, than those who engage in heterosexual behavior. There are several sociobiological explanations of this phenomenon. The one that I shall discuss is similar in structure to the above explanation of the persistence of sickle-cell anaemia: that is, persons heterozygous with respect to a homosexuality allele are more fit than either homozygote (they might, for example, have a higher libido and, hence, leave more offspring than either homozygote). Hence, homosexuality persists in populations because in heterozygotes the allele does not result in homosexual behavior and it confers on its bearer a selective advantage over homozygotes for nonhomosexual behavior.

There are, as the critics have pointed out, several problems with this explanation.[2] The problem relevant to this discussion concerns the ungrounded assumption of a genetic basis to homosexual behavior. This problem is an instance of a more general problem, namely, that underlying sociobiological explanations of behavior is the *assumption* that there is a genetic basis to the behavior being explained. And, in the case of human behavior, this assumption frequently is ungrounded, as it is with this sociobiological explanation of homosexual behavior. The lack of grounding, however, is not, as the critics have claimed, a result of a lack of evidence, but is a result of the absence of other theories required for the theory's application to human behavior. The homosexuality case illustrates this as follows.

The sociobiological explanation of the persistence of homosexual behavior (which is taken to be deleterious from an evolutionary point of view) involves an application of sociobiological theory to homosexual behavior by means of an assumed causal sequence of other theories. This causal sequence of theories is quite similar to the one employed in applying evolutionary theory to sickle-cell anaemia and the explanation of its persistence. It is also required in this case for the same reasons as the causal sequence of theories was required in the sickle-cell case.

The important difference between the two cases is that a promissory note instead of the required theories is offered in the homosexual case, whereas the required theories are available in the sickle-cell case. In other words, there is no physiological theory that causally relates physiological states and behaviors to homosexual behavior, and in the absence of such a theory, the genotype cannot be related to the required physiological states and their behavior because the relevant states cannot be identified. How serious is this problem?

One might be tempted to point out that the sickle-cell anaemia case is unusual. It is rare that such a complete causal account of the physiological states can be given in terms of molecular genetical states by reference to molecular genetical and biochemical theory. In addition, it is seldom the case that more than a sketch of a causal account of a physical condition can be given in terms of physiological states and the behavior of physiological systems. Hence, it might appear that the demands being made on sociobiological explanation are overly stringent. There is, however, a good reason why this is not so.

Although it is seldom the case that complete causal accounts can be given for any of the stages in the causal sequences employed in applying a theory to phenomena, in most cases there is at least a widely accepted theoretical framework which grounds the sketchy causal accounts, provides direction to attempts to flesh out the accounts, and provides a basis for assessing the relevance of experimental data to the account.

Consider, for example, an application of evolutionary theory to anatomical phenomena in order to explain anatomical differences or similarities among populations or species, or to explain a phylogenetic pattern of anatomical development. This application will involve a causal sequence of theories among which will be molecular genetical theory and embryological theory (or theories). Nothing even approaching a complete causal account of the relation between adult anatomy and the zygote is possible, but the theoretical framework(s) provided by embryology grounds the sketchy accounts that can be given, provides direction to attempts to expand the accounts, and provides a framework for assessing the relevance of experimental data. Other cases (such as the molecular genetical one) will be similar.

In the case of human behavior, however, we do not have a widely accepted theoretical framework relating human behaviors, like homosexuality, to physiological states and their behavior. If we did, molecular genetical theory would then serve the above-mentioned functions in causally relating the physiological states and their behavior to molecular genetical states and their behavior. Although certain human behaviors have been related, by current physiological theory, to physiological states (e.g., wake and sleep patterns; see Saunders 1977 and Moore-Ede et al. 1982, the vast array of social and individual human behaviors cannot be related even in a sketchy way to physiological states by reference to current physiological theory. Indeed, unlike most human behavior, sleeping and waking are manifestations of neural activities in the way that sickle-cell anaemia is a manifestation of oxygen deprivation to cells. Current physiological theory describes systems in which these outcomes are a function of physiological states and behaviors. Current physiological theory does not specify systems in which homosexuality, writing articles, and so forth are a function of physiological states and behaviors (though, as I indicate below, some cases of aggressive behavior, along with a limited number of other behaviors, may be able, in current physiological theory, to be related to physiological states). Perhaps in the future current theories of physiology will be expanded, revised, or replaced so that an adequate theory will be available. At present no such theory exists. It is this problem, not the sketchiness of the accounts, that makes the application of sociobiological theory to human behavior methodologically suspect.

In the case of insect behavior and a considerable amount of animal behavior, however, current physiological theory does specify systems which have these behaviors as outcomes of physiological states and behaviors. This is because the behavior of animals discussed by sociobiologists is quite clearly the outcome of physiological states and behaviors of the endocrine system, neurological system, or some other physiological system. Consider, for example, Wilson's discussion of hormones and aggression (Wilson 1975, p. 251):

> The endocrine system of vertebrates acts as a relatively coarse tuning device for the adjustment of aggressive behavior. The interaction of the several hormones in this control are complicated . . . However, they can be understood readily if the entire system is viewed as comprising three levels of controls: the first determines the state of preparedness (androgen, estrogen and luteinizing hormone). . . . The level of preparedness to fight is what we usually refer to as aggressiveness, in order to contrast it with the act of aggression. Aggressiveness, as Rothballer (1967) has said, is a threshold. It can be measured either by the amount of the provoking stimulus required to elicit the act or by the intensity and prolongation of the act in the face of a given stimulus. The class of hormones most consistently associated in the vertebrates with heightened aggression is the androgens, which are 19-carbon steroids, with methyl groups at C-10 and C-13, secreted by the Leydig cells of the testes. Aggression in this account is like withdrawing one's hand when it is pricked by a sharp object. There is a stimulus which elicits a neurological process which results in muscle contraction which results in the behavior of withdrawing the hand. In the case of aggression, there is a stimulus which elicits an endocrine process already primed to go under such stimuli which results in physiological changes which result in aggressive behavior.

No doubt some aspects of human aggression can be placed within this framework, since, like other vertebrates, we have the same hormonal processes as are involved in animal aggression. Most human behaviors, however, are not readily able to be fitted into such physiological accounts, whereas insect behavior and a considerable amount of animal behavior can be so fitted. Even in the case of aggression, human aggression is considered to be substantially more complex, involving factors not amenable to physiological explanation. As indicated above, the central difference between humans and insects appears to be that human behavior involves features that are not capable of being related to physiological states. It may be that this difference will, in the future, be shown illusory. For now, however, it remains an important difference between the two cases—a difference which affects the application of the theory to phenomena. Having now outlined the character of the problem, let me draw the threads together in some concluding remarks.

There are several results which emerge from this discussion. First, the discussion locates the problems outlined by the critics of sociobiology as problems with the application of the theory to humans and not, as the critics have claimed, with the theory itself. This makes intelligible the fact that the theory seems to explain very successfully a wide range of animal behaviors but is much less successful, if at all successful, in explaining human behavior. If the problem is with the theory, as the critics claim, then it is difficult to understand just why the theory is so successful in nonhuman contexts. If, however, the problem is with the application of the theory to phenomena such that, in the case of humans, other theories required in order to apply sociobiological theory to human behavior are not available, whereas, in the case of animals, they very frequently are available, the differences in explanatory success are easily accounted for.

Second, the discussion, by making clear the nature of at least one problem with human sociobiology, makes clear that what is needed are theories that relate human behavior to physiology. And this point makes clear the limitations of human sociobiology without denying the scientific status of the theory and without denying that some human behaviors may be explainable by reference to sociobiological theory. In other words, whenever theories which relate human behavior to genetically based physiological processes exist or become available, sociobiological explanation will be possible. Whenever no such theory exists or other theories exist which relate the behavior to physiological processes which are related by other theories to environmental (broadly understood) factors and not to genes, then no sociobiological explanation will be possible.

The general point about the need for a genetic basis to be established is consequently placed in a different light by making clear that this is not a defect of the theory but of its application, and by making clear that what is needed is not simply more evidence but other theories which are quite independent of sociobiological theory. The success in applying sociobiol200gcal theory to insects indicates the scientific value of the theory and constitutes the arena of testability. The inability to apply it to much of human behavior indicates the limitations of its application. It does not, however, indicate that the theory is untestable and unscientific, but only that human behavior is not a fruitful arena of testing and, at present, cannot be adequately explained by the theory.

Third, the above discussion, by drawing out some of the complexities involved in sociobiological explanations of human behavior, has illustrated the richness of semantic accounts of theory structure and the more thoroughgoing analysis of explanation and testibility that they make possible.

6.2. Intelligence-based Behavior

In the previous section almost no reference was made to behaviors in which cognitive processes play a role. Hormonally driven behaviors, which are almost certainly present in humans, are very different from behaviors which are the result of deliberation or learning. In this section I discuss some of the logical and methodological features of evolutionary explanations of intellegence-based human behavior. Hence, the main thrust of the section will be theoretical, attempting to set out the conceptual role and importance of theories of cognition and neurobiology in applying evolutionary theory to the explanation of human behavior. The main thesis of this section is similar to that of the previous section, namely, that evolutionary explanations of human behavior involve complex causal chains whose links are justified by reference to numerous quite distinct theoretical frameworks.

Among these theoretical frameworks are theories of cognitive psychology and neurobiology that connect cognition to behavior, and theories of cultural transmission of information and behavior patterns. My central goal is to provide a theoretical framework for understanding the need for, and the logic and methodology underlying, such causal chains.

I shall argue that many of the methodological problems with human sociobiology and the abundance of ad hoc hypotheses in sociobiological explanations of human behavior are a result of inadequate attention to the need for theories of cognitive psychology and neurobiology as part of causal chains which link evolutionary theory to phenomena. Indeed, although I shall not concentrate on them, theories from various social sciences are usually required in adequate causal chains. I suggest that the inadequate attention to these causal chains in theoretical discussions is, in large part, due to wide acceptance of the syntactic conception of theories, in which these causal chains play no role in relating a principal theory to phenomena. I shall argue that the semantic conception of theories, because it provides a richer account of the relation of theories to phenomena, including the need for causal chains of imported theories, provides a richer and more methodologically sound account of intelligence-based behavior.

As I have indicated numerous times in other chapters, evolutionary theory involves heredity, variability, and selection (see Lewontin 1974; Sober 1981). All three components are necessary for evolutionary change to occur. Without variation there is no possibility of directional selection. Without selection there is no exploitation of variability, and hence no nonrandom alteration of the phenotype and, consequently, of the genetic structure of populations. Though there are other mechanisms of population change (random drift, for example), selection remains of prime importance. However, although selection will alter the phenotypic structure of a population, unless characteristics are heritable there will be no effect of this selection on subsequent generations. Heredity, therefore, is a necessary component. Hence, any biological evolutionary account of phenomena will involve an establishment of a genetic basis for the phenomena. This is one place where human sociobiology runs into methodological trouble. I have argued in chapter 3 that since there is no unified theory describing the mechanisms of all three of these components, no syntactic conception account of the structure of evolutionary theory is possible. This absence of a syntactic conception account has resulted in severe constraints on the nature and scope of the available responses to conceptual and methodological problems with evolutionary theory and sociobiology.

Cases of 'fixed action patterns' of behavior as found in arthropods and cases of threat and courtship displays in vertebrates are cases where evolutionary explanations are widely accepted and uncontroversial. The reason for this acceptance is that these behaviors are known to have a genetic basis and are, in the main, unaffected by learning, practice, problem-solving abilities, and so forth.

For example, the success of the sociobiological explanation of the ostensibly altruistic behavior of hymenoptera (honey bees) in terms of heterozygote superiority results from the fact that the behavior and it persistence are a function of genes and not of cognitive processes or of culture, which requires the presence of specific cognitive process. In effect, it is a fixed action pattern. Given this feature, Hamilton's coefficient of genetic relationship allows the application of the laws of modern population genetics and selection theory to be employed in a deduction of the apparently altruistic behavior.

Problems arise, however, in cases of behaviors that are not known to have a genetic basis or that are substantially affected by learning, practice, problem-solving abilities, and so forth—in short, by cognitive abilities. These cognitive capacities allow a significant cultural component and personality component to affect behavior and also allow the cultural transmission of behavior patterns from generation to generation.

Almost all human behavior is affected by cognitive capacities. Consequently, evolutionary explanations of human behavior will be complex, and simple explanations patterned after explanations of fixed action patterns will be methodologically inadequate. Not surprisingly, a common tactic of critics who see sociobiology as offering explanations of human behavior patterned on explanations of fixed action patterns is to argue that human sociobiology is, in effect, a biological determinist view within which culture plays no significant role. Frequently, a presupposition of this criticism is that if the role of culture is taken seriously, human sociobiology, with its need to establish a genetic basis for the behaviors it is to explain, will simply cease to be tenable.

This presupposition, I shall argue, is incorrect. If, however, one is constrained by adherence to a syntactic conception of theory structure, the position can appear to have considerable force, because in order to explain a particular human behavior one must be able to *deduce* the behavior from the laws of evolutionary theory. However, behaviors that are significantly affected by learning, practice, problem solving, and so forth are not linked to genes in the direct way required to give a deductive explanation using evolutionary theory alone. Instead, cognitive capacities intervene to modify or radically alter whatever genetic links there might be.

The central problem is that evolutionary theory does not contain either the concepts or the laws of cognitive psychology, neurobiology, or any of the social sciences which are required to deduce behaviors that are significantly affected by cognitive abilities. For example, in the altruistic case discussed above, if there were a significant component of learning involved in the altruistic behavior of hymenoptera, explanation in terms of evolutionary theory *alone* would be impossible, since no deduction from the laws of population genetics, ecology, and selection theory (the component parts of evolutionary theory) would be possible. What is absent from evolutionary theory but necessary to provide, by the deductive method of explaining in the syntactic conception, an account of learned behavior is a theory of the neuropsychology or neurobiology which will specify the effects, if any, of certain patterns and structures of learning on behavior. In addition, some theory of cultural transmission of learned patterns is required.

This significant role of cognitive abilities and culture in human behavior (as well as much animal behavior) and the impossibility of deducing behaviors so affected from the laws of evolutionary theory have caused many biologists, anthropologists, and philosophers to reject human sociobiology as irredeemably flawed methodologically. Its usefulness and acceptability are at best considered to be in the realm of fixed action patterns of behavior and behaviors which are in large part hormonally driven, like threat and courtship patterns: that is, when a direct genetic basis for the behavior can be found or when the behavior is not significantly affected by cognitive abilities. In an attempt to meet these criticisms, Charles Lumsden and Edward O. Wilson (Lumsden and Wilson 1981, 1983), and Michael Ruse (Ruse 1986; Ruse and Wilson 1986) have attempted to introduce the concept of epigenetic rules which constrain but do not dictate behavior. And in a recent paper Lumsden and Gushurst (Lumsden and Gushurst 1986) have made extremely clear the need to take the role of culture very seriously (see section 7.2 below.)

Although pointing in the right direction, the introduction of epigenetic rules still fails to adequately take account of the role of cognitive abilities and culture because it does not provide a theoretical basis for understanding the nature and mechanics of the epigenetic rules. Its fundamental failure is its apparent adherence to the syntactic conception while not providing even a sketch of the deductive character of explanations that the conception requires. This is not surprising, since such a deduction will involve reference to many disparate theories, and in the syntactic conception this is not logically possible because different theories will have unique correspondence rules which will result in unique global meaning for the theory. What is needed is a conception of theories that provides a logical framework within which a number of theories can all contribute to the explanation of a phenomenon.

What emerges, then, is that the natural way to understand the relationship between evolutionary theory and human behavior is in terms of the evolution of neurological structures which *determine* cognitive abilities. Behavior, although not determined by the neurological structures, is constrained and shaped by them. A methodologically adequate explanation will have to account for behavior within these constraints but also in terms of theories about cognition and culture (including the cultural transmission of information and modes of behavior). Hence, theories of cognitive psychology and theories of neurobiology are important to our understanding of the relationship of evolutionary theory to behavior, as are theories about the formation and transmission of information and patterns of behavior through cultural mechanisms.

The schema, consequently, of the relationship between evolutionary theory and human behavior is that evolutionary theory is related to human behavior through a causal chain of theoretical frameworks. Hence, the content and nature of the relationship of evolutionary theory to human behavior is integrally dependent on theories of cognitive psychology, neurobiology, and cultural transmission and the formation of information and patterns of behavior. This kind of multiple-theory type of explanation is precisely what the promising accounts of Robert Boyd and Peter J. Richerson (Richerson and Boyd 1978; Boyd and Richerson 1985), and Henry Plotkin and F. J. Odling-Smee (Plotkin and Odling-Smee 1981) attempt to provide. The major problem for explanations of this kind, in a syntactic conception of theories, is that the relationship of a theory to phenomena is deductive and is specified by the theory itself, and there is therefore no method of employing other theories in relating the theory to phenomena. What is needed is a theoretical framework within which a multiple number of theories can be employed in conjunction in explaining phenomena. This is exactly what the semantic account of theories provides.

In a semantic conception, the relationship of a theory to phenomena is not specified by theory, and a multitude of other theories can be employed in relating the principal theory to phenomena. For example, in a semantic conception, other theories can be employed to account for the fact that the asserted isomorphism of the system specified by the theory and a phenomenal system fails to obtain. This will sometimes be the role played by theories of cognitive psychology, neurobiology, and culture in the sociobiological application of evolutionary theory to human behavior. The effect of cognitive capacities and cultural transmission of information and patterns of behavior is to radically alter the effects that the genes have on behavior. And theories of cognitive psychology, neurobiology, and culture provide a basis for explaining the nature and mechanisms of these alterations.

Consider two simple examples of this kind of role for imported theories. Population-genetical theory describes a breeding system, the principal laws of which are Mendel's law of independent assortment and his law of segregation and the related Hardy-Weinberg equilibrium. A wide array of populations of organisms, including humans, are held to be systems of this kind. However, because of crossing over, linkage, inversion, translocation, and a whole host of other factors, almost no population behaves exactly the way a Mendelian system, as specified by the theory, behaves. What is needed here is a theory about linkage, inversions, translocations, and so forth that specifies the effects these phenomena will have on the structure of actual populations. In this case the theoretical grounding comes from cytological theory and molecular genetics.

The relationship between population genetics and cytological theory is best understood as follows. Cytological theory, neither the terms of which nor the laws of which are part of population genetics, is employed in applying (relating) population genetics to phenomenal systems (populations of organisms). By employing cytological theory, population genetics can be related in a mediated way to populations, and this is possible even though no direct deduction, as required by the syntactic conception, of certain phenomena from population genetics alone is possible, since phenomena are affected by cytological factors which are not described by population genetics. What cytological theory does, in effect, is to provide a basis for asserting that actual populations are systems of the kind described by population genetics even though there are clear differences in the behavior of the two systems. It does this by providing accounts of linkage, translocation, and so forth which make clear that the differences between the systems are not a result of the inapplicability of the theory to the particular phenomena but of other causal factors described by other theories.

In a similar way, the relation between evolutionary theory and human behavior is mediated by theories of cognitive psychology, neurobiology, and culture. These theories provide a theoretical grounding for the differences in the way the system specified by evolutionary theory behaves and the way phenomenal systems (i.e., human individuals and societies) behave. The differences in this case are a result of the effects of learning, problem solving abilities, and so forth, the nature and effects of which are the subject of theories of cognitive psychology, neurobiology, and culture.

Though there are differences in content, the logic of the genetic cytology case and that of the sociobiological case are identical. In the genetic cytology case, the behavior of chromosomes is genetically based and hence amenable to evolutionary explanation. However, cytological theory is an important part of the explanatory application of population genetics to actual populations of organisms. In the case of sociobiology, the nature and extent of cognitive abilities are a product of evolution and hence amenable to evolutionary explanation. However, and this is the crucial point, theories of cognitive psychology and neurobiology about the nature of human cognitive abilities and about their effects on human behavior are important to applying evolutionary theory to human behavior. Without theories of cognitive psychology, the application of evolutionary theory to human behavior is as methodologically and logically flawed as the attempt to apply population genetics to the behavior of actual populations without reference to cytology.

The upshot of this is that, in the syntactic conception, the failure of the phenomena to be deducible from the theory has but two remedies: rejection of the theory—a drastic and seldom employed remedy if no alternative theory is available—or the development of ad hoc hypotheses which will permit the deduction of the phenomena. The latter was the route taken by FitzGerald and Lorentz when faced by the null result of the Michelson-Morley experiment. Since the results indicated a discrepancy between the actual phenomena under investigation and what could be derived from Newtonian mechanics, Fitz-Gerald and Lorentz (independently) proposed the ad hoc hypotheses that a body contracted in the direction of its travel through the ether. Indeed, this technique is resorted to frequently when the phenomena cannot be deduced from the laws of a theory as understood in a syntactic conception.

What has happened in the case of sociobiology is that its strongest critics have, in the face of the fact that there are obvious difficulties in deducing human behavior from evolutionary theory, advocated the reject-the-theory resolution. Sociobiologists, on the other hand, have chosen to resolve this problem by developing ad hoc hypotheses (e.g., the multiplier effect,—some of which are more plausible than others. These hypotheses are ad hoc because they are not derivable from the axioms of the theory, nor are they axioms of the theory. They are nonintegrated "add-ons" to the theory, their sole purpose being to allow the deduction of phenomena.

What I have been pressing for is a rejection not of sociobiology, but of the conception of theories that makes it appear as if there are only these two options, and I have been arguing in favor of the richer and more descriptively accurate semantic conception of theories. In a semantic conception, evolutionary theory encompasses a number of specifications of systems, the laws of which are those of population genetics, selection, molecular genetics, and ecology. Actual populations are held to be systems of the kind jointly specified by these theories. Faced with discrepancies between the two systems, one can opt for a different, I think preferable, methodological solution, namely, the employment of other theories from different but relevant domains that provide a theoretical, and not ad hoc, account of the nature of the discrepancies and a method of resolving them. And that is the solution I have been pressing for in this section.

This solution is possible in a semantic conception because the relationship between theories and phenomena is not deductive. The deductive component is one of deducing states of the system on the basis of laws which specify the behavior of the system. The relationship between the theory and phenomena is one of asserted structural behavioral and identity, an assertion which is to be empirically tested. This testing will involve careful applications of theories of experimental design and data analysis as well as other theories which will often indicate why the phenomenal system seems to behave differently than the system specified by the theory.

Therefore, I submit that it is the adherence to a conception of theory structure that fails to provide a role for theories of cognitive psychology, neurobiology, and culture in evolutionary explanations of human behavior that has resulted in the methodological and logical heavy weather in which sociobiology has sailed. I suggest that it has also resulted in a level of speculation and ad hoc hypothesis formation that exceeds acceptable bounds. The speculation and ad hoc hypothesis formation have been a substitute for a logical role for theories of cognitive pyschology, neurobiology, and culture which have not been employed where they are clearly required. And the failure to see the need and nature of their employment is a function of adherence to a syntactic conception of theory structure.

What I have been arguing in this chapter is that the methodological and logical problems with human sociobiology can be clearly identified and remedied by changing the conception of theory structure being employed to formalize the theory and its relationship to phenomena. The alternative conception of theory structure that I am promoting in this book makes clear the methodological and logical role of other theories in applying evolutionary theory to phenomena. In particular, it makes clear the logical and methodological role of (as well as the necessity for) theories of cognitive psychology, of neurobiology, and of the cultural transmission and formation of information and patterns of behavior in applying evolutionary theory to human behavior.

This is something that is entirely absent from the syntactic conception of theory structure but is crucial to a logically and methodically sound human sociobiology (as well as many other theoretical domains). Far from preempting the social sciences, sociobiology must make significant use of them in causal explanatory chains which link evolutionary theory to human behavior.

Notes

1. Consider, for example, Gould's claim: "Most of *Sociobiology* wins from me the same high praise almost universally accorded to it. For a lucid account of evolutio-

nary principles and an indefatigably thorough discussion of social behavior among all groups of animals, *Sociobiology* will be the primary document for years to come. But Wilson's last chapter, 'From Sociobiology to Sociology', leaves me very unhappy indeed. After twenty-six chapters of careful documentation for the non-human animals, Wilson concludes with an extended speculation on the genetic basis of supposedly universal patterns of human behavior" (Gould 1976, p. 344).

2. For example, it is not clear that there is a phenomenon to be explained. Unless all (or at least most) homosexuals have exclusively homosexual encounters, there is no phenomenon of the persistence of an apparently deleterious behavior to be explained sociobiologically. If even 25 percent of dispositional homosexuals engaged in heterosexual activity frequently enough to leave offspring, there would be no mystery about the persistence of the behavior, even granting its genetic basis. Hence, given that there is no clear evidence on this matter, sociobiologists cannot be sure that an evolutionary explanation is necessary or approprate. In addition, there are good reasons for believing that there are considerable social influences on homosexual behavior, since, as Lewontin has pointed out, there is known to be an "immense variation in the frequency of homosexual and heterosexual behavior in history and between social classes" (Lewontin 1977, p. 28).

CHAPTER 7

Culture and the Evolutionary Process: Multitheoretic and Multilevel Explanatory Causal Chains

I provide in this chapter, in a brief way, a programmatic sketch of how two other promising areas of foundational work in evolutionary biology are more faithfully represented in a semantic conception than in a syntactic conception and how the syntactic conception provides a more thoroughgoing and richer account of the complexity of the theorizing. These two areas of foundational work involve exploring two fundamental questions of philosophy from within an evolutionary framework. It is not my intention to resolve important controversies in either of these areas, but rather to indicate the important gains to be made in understanding the logic of theorizing in these areas in a semantic conception. Indeed, I maintain that the level of complexity required for anything like an adequate evolutionary expistemology or evolutionary ethics to be possible makes adherence to a semantic conception mandatory.

7.1. Evolutionary Epistemology

The implications of evolutionary theory for a theory of knowledge have been explored in the period since Darwin by numerous writers. In general, these writers have developed theories about the development of knowledge by analogy with evolutionary theory: that is, they have developed theories which apply the mechanism of differential selection on variation to the growth of knowledge. In this sense knowledge is seen to be a function of success (often understood in pragmatic terms) in a field of alternative ideas. Knowledge evolves in much the same way as organisms. Hence the title *evolutionary epistemology*. This evolutionary epistemology has, in various forms, been espoused and developed by Stephen Toulmin, Karl Popper, Donald Campbell, and others.

What I have called the "new" evolutionary epistemology differs from these analogical approaches in that it emphasizes that human knowledge is *literally* a product of Darwinian evolution: that is, human knowledge is a function, in important respects, of our biology. And, since our biology is a product of evolution, the nature of our knowledge must also be a product of evolution.

Hence human knowledge must be explained within an evolutionary framework. This conception of evolutionary epistemology is most prominent in sociobiological theorizing, with Richard Dawkins, Charles Lumsden, Edward O. Wilson, and Michael Ruse being among its strongest proponents.

For example, in his latest book, *Taking Darwin Seriously*, Michael Ruse has produced an outline of an evolutionary epistemology in this sense that is firmly planted within the context of sociobiological theorizing along the lines of Dawkins and Wilson. According to Ruse, we can take Darwin seriously by recognizing that we are biological entities that have been shaped by evolution in more ways than physiologically. In addition to physiology, ethics and epistemology have a clear evolutionary determinant. The ways in which we think and our problem-solving strategies have arisen at least in part because they made survival possible.

This literal application of evolutionary theory to theoretical work on epistemology is long overdue. However, one must not incautiously believe that just because the explanation of epistemology must take place in an evolutionary context, evolutionary theory is all that is required in order to explain human knowledge. It is not. As indicated in chapter 1, David Hull quite correctly remarked that

> certain advocates of evolutionary epistemology seem to propose a literal extension of the theory of biological evolution to cover sociocultural phenomena. I happen to think that much more about the behavior traits and social organization of *Homo sapiens* is going to be explicable in strictly biological terms than most of us would like, in particular those traits most closely connected to reproduction. I disagree with those authors who seem to think that such an extension of evolutionary theory is *a priori* impossible. However, I also think that no strictly biological theory is going to explain everything about human sociocultural development, in particular it is not going to explain very much about the changes in the *content* of human conceptual systems. (Hull 1982, p. 274)

It is, of course those changes that play an important part in cognition.

In this discussion I shall take Darwin seriously in the way suggested by Ruse: that is, I shall take seriously the fact that any explanation of the nature of human knowledge and any theoretical account of the way in which knowledge is acquired must have an integral evolutionary component. I shall argue, however, that much more than evolutionary theory is needed in order to have an adequate theoretical account of the nature and acquisition of human knowledge. In addition, for example, some account of the mechanisms of cultural information transmission is necessary as well as an account of the ways in which information transmitted culturally affects the acquisition of knowledge. I shall argue that, in effect, an adequate theoretical account of human knowledge requires the employment of a number of different theoretical frameworks in an interactive way. Consequently, explanations of epistemology within an evolutionary context will involve complex theoretical frameworks.

The remainder of the section will concentrate on the logical, conceptual, and methodological features of the interaction among the various theoretical domains which interactively constitute the theoretical framework for an adequate evolutionary epistemology. I shall argue, as throughout this book, that the syntactic conception of theories is, and has been, a stumbling block to any formal understanding of the logic of complex theorizing of this kind. A more useful conception of theories for these complex cases is a semantic conception.

The basic argument underlying the "new" evolutionary epistemology is that the method by which organisms acquire and process information as well as any specific propensities to hold certain beliefs must be selectively advantageous to those organisms in relevant environments. Methods of acquiring and processing information that led organisms to interact with their environments in ways that were detrimental to their survival had a decreasing representation in subsequent generations. Hence, knowledge acquisition and processing are a product of evolution and need to be understood and explained in terms of evolutionary theory.

This is not to say that culture plays no role. For Dawkins, the 'meme' is a unit of information which is "a completely non-genetic kind of replicator, which flourishes only in the environment provided by complex communicating brains" (Dawkins 1982, p. 109) 'Meme's are, in effect, culturally transmitted. For Lumsden and Wilson gene and culture are "inseverably linked" (Lumsden and Wilson 1983, p. 117), resulting in gene-culture coevolution. In their view, genetically prescribed rules of development (epigenetic rules) assemble the mind in ways which allow culture to be absorbed and in which the differential success of the rules in absorbing culture and in participating in changing culture in ways that increase fitness will cause the genes, and hence the rule they prescribe, to evolve. Ruse, who has most consciously attempted to address logical and conceptual aspects of the "new" evolutionary epistemology, tends to identify with Lumsden's and Wilson's view.

Neither of these attempts to give culture a role is entirely adequate. 'Memes' are culturally transmitted, and insofar as a meme provides a selective advantage to an organism, it provides a selective advantage to the gene which determines the brain structure in which that meme was capable of being encoded. As I hope to indicate in a moment, however, this is not a rich enough framework to allow for the kind of complex interaction that occurs between genetically determined brain structures and cultural information.

The brain is not just a storage unit for environmental and culturally transmitted information; it is what it is because of environmental and culturally transmitted information. Wilson's and Lumsden's gene-culture coevolution, as expressed in Lumsden and Wilson 1981, takes even less seriously the extent to which environmental and culturally transmitted information and not just epigenetic rules determine the nature of cognition. It should be noted, however, that movement toward a more serious treatment of these determinants occurs in their later and more accessible work (Lumsden and Wilson 1983) and in Lumsden's recent work (see Lumsden and Gushurst 1986). The general thrust of these later works is consistant with the position I develop in this section and the next. Indeed, the open sentences of the Lumsden and Gushurst paper express exactly the position I adopt: "Human beings were not created by biological Darwinian evolution. For the past several million years our ancestors have been shaped by biological evolution and cultural evolution proceeding together in a manner still little understood." (Lumsden and Gushurst 1986, p. 3).

What these accounts, until very recently, have not given adequate weight to is the complex interaction of the structural properties of the neurological material and the environmental and culturally transmitted information that results in cognition and cognitive abilities. A great deal can be learned in the context of evolutionary epistemology by taking seriously recent work in cognitive psychology and artificial intelligence. I shall in this chapter only sketch the richer, more adequate account of cognition that I think can be gleaned from work in cognitive science. The essence of this account is that human cognition is analogous in complexity to computer cognition and that part of this complexity can be seen in the interrelation of the hardware and the software in computer cognition.

The human analogue to hardware and software is the neurological structure of the brain and the environmental programming of that structure. The environmental programming occurs through direct trial and error experience but more substantially, in the case of human cognition, through teaching. Included in teaching is both verbal and nonverbal communication of information. Information includes techniques of problem solving as well as data. The information taught is a cultural heritage which is culturally transmitted and evolves.

Much of the work of the past decade or so on artificial intelligence and computer simulation has increased our understanding of the sort of framework of interaction that I am suggesting occurs between the neurological hardware and the software which is in part supplied by the learning of culturally transmitted information. Computer simulation and artifical intelligence differ in that computer simulation is an attempt to write a program functionally equivalent to a psychological theory, whereas artificial intelligence is a more general attempt to write a program that can achieve a specified goal quite independently of whether humans or any other organism does it that way. For the purposes of exploring the interaction between culturally transmitted information and a genetically specified neurological system this distinction can be ignored.

A computer program is a series of instructions which when given to a machine structured to accept instructions in that language will constitute an "effective procedure." The series of instructions which make up the program in effect specify the nature of the information processing which can be performed by the machine. The machine—the hardware—needs a program in order that higher-level languages (English, for example) can be used to communicate with it. A number of differentially appropriate programming languages exist which allow this communication with the machine in a higher-level language. Some of those most frequently used in work on artificial intelligence and computer simulation are LISP and PROLOG; FORTRAN, CONNIVER, and others are used considerably less frequently.

What I am suggesting is that human cognition involves interactions at least as complex as those involved in computer cognition. I have no desire to defend the thesis that the details of human cognition are similar to those of a computer. The position I am developing is quite general: human cognition consists of features analogous to a computer's hardware and software. The neurological structures are the hardware which, as with a computer, comes prewired to accept instructions of a particular kind. It has a prewired logic. How much problem-solving ability is prewired is as yet not known. But quite clearly individuals learn quite high-level problem-solving strategies from others within the culture. Hence, significant problem-solving abilities can be taken to be a result of cultural programming. Cultural teaching can then be seen as analogous to programming software.

Exactly how culturally transmitted information interacts with the genetically transmitted neurological hardware is the subject of the growing field of cognitive science of which work on artificial intelligence and computer simulation is a part. Theories of cognitive science also encompass psychological theorizing about learning. Hence, this is quite naturally the disciplinary complex to which one looks for theories about the interaction of culturally transmitted information and genetically transmitted neurological systems.

This sketch of one aspect of the complexity of human cognition makes clear the role of evolutionary theory in an account of cognition. Evolution has brought about the neurological structure. And an explanation of its development will involve reference to the mechanisms of evolutionary theory, including fitness. What the sketch also makes clear is that evolutionary theory is not sufficient in accounting for human cognition. In addition, at least two other theoretical frameworks are required. First, a theory of nongenetic transmission of information is necessary. Second, a theory of cognition which encompasses the way in which cultural information programs the neurological system or in some other way interacts with it is necessary.

An extremely promising begining to the development of a theory of cultural transmission has been put forward by Robert Boyd and Peter J. Richerson in several articles and most recently in their book *Culture and the Evolutionary Process (1985)*. In their book, they explore several different models of cultural inheritance. They argue (1) "that empirical work in the social sciences supports the notion that social learning in the human species has the properties of an inheritance system"; and (2) that "this qualitative description of cultural transmission could be translated, albeit in a stylized way, into mathematical models" which "at least in principle, allow us to deduce the long-run, population-level consequences of particular forms of cultural transmission" (pp. 79–80).

I now turn to a discussion of the ways in which conceptions of the structure of scientific theories are relevant to understanding and representing complex theorizing of which evolutionary epistemology is an example. I have suggested above in this section that an adequate account of the nature and method of knowledge acquisition by humans involves the interaction of three quite different theoretical domains: evolutionary theory, cognitive science, and a theory of cultural transmission. A theory of cultural transmission provides the causal framework for understanding and explaining the cumulative development of nongenetic information and information-processing techniques. Cognitive science provides the causal framework for understanding and explaining how information is processed and stored and how nongenetically transmitted information and information-processing techniques affect cognition. Evolutionary theory provides the causal framework for understanding and explaining the cumulative development of the hardware (neurology) of cognition. These theories are almost certainly not enough. Theories of embryology, for example, will also play an important role in understanding the nature of the hardware. But although not enough, the three that I have concentrated on in this section do provide a considerably richer account than any one of them alone can do, and the complex view which emerges points in the right direction and makes great strides towards a more adequate view.

The problem with Ruse's evolutionary epistemology is that it is formulated within a syntactic conception of theory structure. The central problem with adherence to this conception is that it renders impossible the integration of multiple numbers of theories within a causal explanatory framework. This is a function of the fact that, in the syntactic conception, the relationship of a theory to phenomena is deductive and is specified by the theory itself, and there is, therefore, no method of employing other theories in relating the theory to phenomena. In the case of evolutionary theory, since it does not contain the laws of cognitive psychology or of cultural transmission, deduction of phenomena, like knowledge acquisition, from it *alone* is not possible. Therefore, it is, I suggest, Ruse's adherence to this conception of theory structure, coupled with his conviction that evolutionary theory ought to be able to explain cognition, that led him to apply evolutionary theory to cognition in exactly the way it is applied to the physical features of organisms. Evolutionary theory *alone*, however, is not rich enough to capture the complexity of cognition. What is needed is a conception of theory structure which accounts for complex theory interactions such that the application of evolutionary theory to cognition employs other theories as links in complex causal chains. This is exactly what the semantic conception provides.

In a semantic conception, the relationship of a theory to phenomena is not specified by the theory, and a multitude of other theories can be employed. For example, in a semantic conception, other theories can be employed to account for the fact that the asserted isomorphism between the physical system specified by the theory and a phenomenal system fails to obtain. This will sometimes be the role played by theories of cognitive science and of cultural transmission in the evolutionary explanation of cognition. The causal effects of processes described by theories of cognitive science and cultural transmission intervene between the genes and actual cognition.

Consider again the example given in chapter 6 of this kind of role for theories. Population genetic theory defines a breeding system, the principle laws of which are Mendel's laws of independent assortment and segregation and the related Hardy-Weinberg equilibrium. A wide array of populations, including humans, are held to be systems of this kind. However, because of crossing over, linkage, inversion, translocation, and a whole host of other factors, almost no population is isomorphic to a Mendelian system. What is needed here in order to understand in exactly what sense populations in a phenomenal system are systems of the kind specified by population genetic theory is a theory about linkage, translocations, and so forth. Such a theory will specify the effects that these phenomena have on the structure of actual populations. In this case the theoretical grounding comes from cytological theory and molecular genetic theory.

The relationship between population genetics and cytology is best understood as follows. Cytological theory, neither the terms of which nor the laws of which are part of population genetics, is employed in applying population genetics to phenomenal systems (i.e., actual populations). By employing cytological theory, population genetics can be related in a mediated way to populations. This highlights one main problem with the syntactic conception. Since neither the terms nor the laws of cytology are part of population genetics, no deduction, as required by the syntactic conception, of the nature of inheritance in actual populations is possible from population genetics alone. Indeed, many of the significant terms and laws of cytology will be meaningless within the context of population genetics because it will contain no correspondence rules for them.

As stated over and over again in this book, in a semantic conception the relationship between a theory and phenomena is not deductive and is not specified by the theory itself. The deductive component is that of deducing the states of a system on the basis of laws which specify the possible configurations of the system, the behavior of the system, and the possible inputs to the system and their effects upon the states of the system. The relationship of a theory to phenomena is not specified by the theory and consists in an assertion that the system specified by the theory is structurally and behaviorally identical to the phenomenal system to which it is applied. Establishing the acceptability of this assertion constitutes a testing of the acceptability of applying the theory to the phenomenal system. This is a complex task requiring the employment of theories of experimental design, goodness of fit, and so forth, as well as other scientific theories. Hence, in a semantic conception, other theories can be employed in relating a theory to phenomena. What in effect results is a causal chain whose links are grounded by appeal to different theories.

The complex theoretical framework that I have suggested is necessary for an adequate evolutionary epistemology is similar to the genetic-cytology example, and the logic of such a framework is the same. Evolutionary theory, theories of cognitive psychology, and theories of cultural inheritance interact to form complex causal explanatory chains, the links of which are grounded by reference to the appropriate theories. In addition, and though important I shall only mention it in passing here, other theories can generate inputs into a system specified by the theory in accordance with the laws of interaction of the theory.

In this section I have attempted to reinforce the position argued for in other chapters that the semantic conception of theories provides a better account of the logic of complex theoretical frameworks. I have concentrated on the way in which it provides an understanding of the interaction of multiple numbers of theories, as well as how it avoids the necessity of emphasizing one theory in the complex at the expense of trivializing or ignoring the role of others. By way of conclusion I offer a diagnosis of the fundamental flaw with the *literal* evolutionary epistemology of Dawkins, Lumsden and Wilson, and Ruse. Their accounts place undue emphasis on one of a number of interacting theories, namely, evolutionary theory. Although some simplification is often necessary in order to reduce complexity, their restricted theoretical framework is largely due to an explicit or tacit adherence to a syntactic and deductive conception of theories. In a syntactic conception one might concede that other aspects are important, but the conception restricts explanation, prediction, and understanding to a single domain of theorizing, and hence distorts the actual interactive complexity.

7.2. Evolutionary Ethics

Although the distinction between 'is' and 'ought' and between 'fact' and 'value' predates Hume, since Hume it has been widely held that values cannot be derived from facts alone. With G. E. Moore (Moore 1903) the fallacy of deriving values from facts was given a name: the naturalistic fallacy. The naturalistic fallacy can be easily demonstrated by providing examples of arguments that purport to derive values from facts and then showing that they are in fact enthymemes (arguments which are incompletely expressed). When the unexpressed premise or premises are uncovered, one or more of them is invariably a premise expressing a value judgement. For example, if one were to support the claim that war is wrong by pointing to the fact that war causes pain and suffering, one would have offered an enthymeme. The claim that war is wrong does not follow from the fact that war causes pain and suffering unless one also accepts the premise that something that causes pain and suffering is wrong. This latter premise, however, does not state a fact but a value judgement.

In light of this fact, the central problem with evolutionary ethics seems to be the inevitability of committing the naturalistic fallacy. If ethics is taken to be grounded in evolution, one is deriving values from facts—facts about the evolution of organisms. In general it is assumed that evolution can tell us how things are and why but cannot tell us how they ought to be. In the same way, even if studies on children provided convincing evidence that aggressive behavior among children is genetic and hence in some sense "natural," this would not entail that children ought to be allowed or encouraged to be aggressive.

With the publication of *Sociobiology: The New Synthesis* (Wilson 1975), the discussion of the evolutionary basis of ethics was reopened. The major thrust of these discussions has been to avoid the naturalistic fallacy by focusing not on the content of right and wrong but on the propensity to develop and adhere to systems of right and wrong. In other words, evolution is not used to derive right and wrong behavior but to explain why humans are interested in behaving in ways that they take to be right and wrong. Explanations given by Wilson and others immediately following the book's publication were complex but ultimately crude. The explanatory models of this period are described by Lumsden and Gushurst (Lumsden and Gushurst 1985, p. 17) as "classical sociobiological models." These models "tend to equate the human moral passions to reactions that are hardwired into the brain's limbic system" (Lumsden and Gushurst 1985, p. 17).

Since, in these models, behavior is "hardwired," what is is what must be. Value, as Lumsden and Gushurst point out, is "ultimately an expression of reproductive and survival advantage" (p. 17). This conclusion results in a redefinition of 'value' such that there is no question of what one ought to do, only what one is biologically disposed to do. But if the values that are being given an evolutionary biological explanation are not the moral values that are part of ethical codes, then moral values have not been explained but simply put aside or denied to have any reality. If they have put aside, all that has been given is an explanation for human behavior and not an evolutionary basis for how humans *ought* to behave. Hence, an evolutionary explanation of ethics would not have been given. This alternative, however, is not the one underlying classical sociobiological models. It is instead the denial that moral values have any reality that underlies these models.

If, however, it is assumed that moral values have no reality, then an independent argument is needed to justify this denial. What is meant by the claim that moral values have no reality is, most frequently, that they have no *objectve, independent* status—in effect, we invent them. What, therefore, is in need of explanation is why we invent the kinds of systems of moral values that we do. The answer in "classical sociobiological models" is straightforward. We invent particular moral systems because they increase our reproductive success. And, since the behaviors examined in these models are assumed to be "hardwired" into the brain's limbic system, a standard evolutionary explanation of why we invent the particular moral systems we do can be given.

There are two important assumptions in this "classical-sociobiological-model" explanation of ethics. The first is the assumption of an independent justification that moral values are not "real." The second is the assumption of a biological determinism expressed in terms of "hardwiring." The second of these assumptions is challenged by current sociobiological models within which culture has been given a greater and greater role. As can be anticipated, given what I have argued in the last two chapters, it is the role of culture in the more mature sociobiological theorizing that makes the semantic view of theories a more appropriate conception for the formal investigation of the logic of this area of sociobiological theorizing. In addition, it is a commitment to the syntactic view that makes explanatory models based on "hardwiring" seem so much more complete and formally satisfying than those that involve an appeal to cultural determinants. Before saying more about this, however, I shall focus briefly on the first assumption regarding the reality of moral values.

The importance of this assumption can be seen in the recent philosophical treatment of evolutionary ethics by Ruse in his book *Taking Darwin Seriously* (Ruse 1986). Ruse attempts to tackle the issue of the naturalistic fallacy ("Hume's law") head on. In his view, "the Darwinian does an end-run around the is/ought barrier. He/she realizes that you cannot go through it, but argues that you can go around it, giving morality all the justificatory insight possible"

(Ruse 1986, p. 256). The end-run that Ruse has in mind involves assuming that ethics is not objective but an invention. Since Ruse shows his hand on this issue quite clearly in two paragraphs and since the structure of his analogical reasoning in those paragraphs is extremely instructive, I think it worthwhile to quote them in full:

> Consider an analogy. During the First World War, many bereaved parents and wives turned to spiritualism for solace. They would try to communicate with the dead, thus numbing their sense of loss. And not a few felt they were successful in their efforts. Down through the ouija board would come reassuring messages: "It's all right, Mum. I've gone to a far better place. I'll be waiting for you and Dad." How do we analyse such messages as these? We can discount universally blatant fraud. I am sure that people (including many of the professional spiritualists) were genuine. I take it that readers will also agree with me that we can exclude the possibility that the fallen were indeed speaking to the survivors. You cannot justify "Don't worry about me" by saying that it was really the late Private Higgins speaking from Beyond. How else do you account for messages received from someone who turns out to be alive and well, but in prison camp? The obvious correct answer is that the bereaved were subconsciously deceiving themselves, because of their extreme psychological anxiety. This is the answer you can give, and all the answer that you need give.
>
> The Darwinian argues that we have a similar situation in ethics. You cannot justify "Killing is wrong" in the sense of deducing it from factual premises. What you can do is explain why we hold this belief. This is all that can or need be offered. The difference between the spiritualism case and morality is that, in the former, most people recognize its deceptive nature and, therefore, we can quite comfortably and literally speak of "illusion." In the case of morality we are all part of the game, and even those of us who realize this have no desire to drop out. (Ruse 1986, pp. 256–257)

Leaving aside questions about the details of the spiritualist example, such as the possibility that a spiritualist could easily explain how the living who were thought dead could communicate through the ouija board, what is clear is that any force that Ruse's explanation of the spiritualist case has is very dependent on the assumption that there is no reality to the supposed phenomenon of communcating with the dead. And Ruse is quite clear that, consistent with the analogy, the Darwinian assumes that there is no real phenomenon of ethics to be explained. In both cases, *all that can and need be* explained is why people believe the phenomenon (communication with the dead and ethics).

The way to avoid the naturalistic fallacy, therefore, is to deny that there are moral values to be deduced from facts, and then to provide an evolutionary explanation to explain why humans believe that there are moral values and choose to behave in accordance with them. In the case of communicating with the dead, however, most people easily accept Ruse's explanation because most people think there are good arguments for denying the reality of communication with the dead. If people did not, evidence and arguments for this view would be demanded. In the case of ethics, however, few are so certain that ethics is an "illusion." Hence, what Ruse and other sociobiologists who wish to explain ethics evolutionarily require is an argument that ethics is an invention of humans and not objectively real. Since few sociobiologists appear to have seen clearly the importance of this premise to their argument or the need for a justification of it, it is never given. Unfortunately, even Ruse, who sees the importance of the premise, does not argue for it. Fortunately, however, an argument that I think is extremely compelling has been given by J. L. Mackie (Mackie 1977). On the strength of Mackie's argument, one central premise of a sociobiological approach to evolutionary ethics is grounded.

I now return to the second assumption of "classical sociobiological models" (i.e., that behavior is "hardwired"). As indicated, this assumption has been rejected within more recent sociobiological theorizing. As Lumsden and Gushurst claim, "Gene-culture theories and their supporting data indicate that the complexity of human ethical behavior is not reducible to genes and hardwired responses" (Lumsden and Gushurst 1986, pp. 17–18). And, as Wilson admits, "hardwiring" excludes conscious choice and the cultural transmission of moral values (see Lumsden and Wilson 1983). Recent sociobiological theorizing recognizes the cognitive capacities of humans and the reality of the cultural transmission of moral values.

Recognition of these features of an adequate evolutionary account of ethics, however, brings with it an increased complexity of the explanatory framework. As was argued in the previous chapter, this complexity is, in part, a function of the need to appeal to a number of different theories in order to produce an adequate account. 'Evolutionary theory' will be applied to the phenomenon in conjunction with theories from anthropology, cognitive psychology, neurobiology, and so forth.

Adherence to a syntactic conception of theory structure will mitigate against such complex accounts because it provides a framework within which theories are independently and directly applied to phenomena. However, as I hope I have by now shown, in a semantic conception the logic of these complex explanatory frameworks can be captured quite faithfully. An analysis of recent work on evolutionary ethics, therefore, provides yet another example of the faithfulness of the semantic conception to foundational work in evolutionary biology and of the richness of this conception in comparison with the syntactic conception.

Conclusion

I have argued that the semantic conception of the structure of scientific theories is more faithful to foundational work in evolutionary biology and provides a richer account of the structure of evolutionary theory and of the relationship of that theory to phenomena. Specifically, I have argued that evolutionary theory is not a unified theory but a family of theories which interactively constitute a framework for explaining, investigating, and integrating evolutionary phenomena. This view of evolutionary theory cannot be accommodated in a syntactic conception but can in a semantic conception. In addition, this view is fundamental to adequate sociobiological theorizing.

Of equal importance to adequate sociobiological theorizing is the more complex understanding in the semantic conception of the ways in which theories relate to the world. This more complex understanding accommodates the complex causal chains involved in explaining phenomena. The links of these chains are grounded in theories other than evolutionary theory. These other theories are essential logical components in the evolutionary explanation or prediction of phenomena.

Not surprisingly, I think that I have provided a compelling case for the acceptance of the semantic conception. Also not surprisingly, there are those who will disagree.

Bibliography

Achinstein, P. (1963) "Theoretical Terms and Partial Intepretation," *British Journal for the Philosophy of Science* 14: 89–105.

_____.(1965) "The Problem with Theoretical Terms," *American Philosophical Quarterly* 2: 193–203.

_____. (1968) *Concepts of Science.* Baltimore: Johns Hopkins Press.

Allen, E., et al (1976) "Sociobiology: Another Biological Determinism," *Bioscience* 26: 182–186.

Ayala, F.J. (1968) "Biology as an Autonomous Science," *American Scientist* 56:207–221.

_____. (1970) "Teleological Explanation in Evolutionary Biology," *Philosophy of Science* 37: 1–15.

_____. (1983) "Beyond Darwinism? The Challenge of Macroevolution to the Synthetic Theory of Evolution." In P.D. Asquith and T. Nickles (eds.), *PSA 1982*, vol. 2. East Lansing, Mich.: Philosophy of Science Association, pp. 275–292.

_____. (1987) "The Biological Roots of Morality," *Biology and Philosophy* 2: 235–252.

Ayala, F.J., and Valentine, J. (1976) *Evolving.* Melano Park, Calif.: Benjamin Cummings.

Beatty, J. (1980) "Optimal-Design Models and the Strategy of Model Building in Evolutionary Biology," *Philosophy of Science* 47: 532–561.

_____. (1981) "What's Wrong with the Received View of Evolutionary Theory?" In P.D. Asquith and R.N. Giere (eds.), *PSA 1980*, vol. 2. East Lansing, Mich.: Philosophy of Science Association.

_____. (1983) "What's in a Word? Coming to Terms in the Darwinian Revolution" In M. Ruse (ed.) *Nature Animated* Dordrecht: Reidel, pp. 79–100.

_____. (1987) "On Behalf of the Semantic View," *Biology and Philosophy* 2: 17–23.

Beckner, M. (1959) *The Biological Way of Thought*, New York: Columbia University Press.

Bergmann, G. (1951) "The Logic of Psychological Concepts," *Philosophy of Science* 18: 93–110.

Bergmann, G., and Spence, K. (1941) "Operationism and Theory in Psychology," *Psychological Review* 48: 1–14.

Beth, E. (1948) *Natuurphilosophie*, Gorinchem: Noorduyn.

_____ . (1949) "Towards an Up-to-Date Philosophy of the Natual Sciences," *Methodos* 1: 178–185.

_____ . (1961) "Semantics of Physical Theories." In H. Freudenthal (ed.), *The Concept and the Role of the Model in Mathematics and Natural and Social Sciences*. Dordrecht: Reidel, pp. 48–51.

Boyd R., and Richerson, P.J. (1985) *Culture and the Evolutionary Process*. Chicago: University of Chicago Press.

Braithwaite, R. (1953) *Scientific Explanation*. Cambridge: Cambridge University Press.

Bromberger, S. (1966) "Why-Questions." In R.G. Colodney (ed.), *Mind and Cosmos: Essays in Contemporary Science and Philosophy*. Pittsburg: University of Pittsburg Press.

Burian, R.M. (1978) "A Methodological Critique of Sociobiology." In A.L. Caplan (ed.), *The Sociobiology Debate*. New York Harper & Row, pp. 376–395.

Caplan, A.L. (ed.) (1978) *The Sociobiology Debate*. New York Harpter & Row.

Carnap, R. (1936) "Testability and Meaning," *Philosophy of Science* 3: 420–468.

_____ . (1937) Testability and Meaning," *Philosophy of Science* 4: 1–40.

_____ . (1939) *Foundations of Logic and Mathematics*. Chicago: University of Chicago Press.

_____ . (1956) "The Methodological Character of Theoretical Concepts." In H. Feigl and M. Scriven (eds.), *Minnesota Studies in the Philosophy of Science*, vol. 1. (Minneapolis: University of Minnesota Press.

_____ . (1966) *An Introduction to the Philosophy of Science*, ed. M. Gardner. New York: Basic Books.

Caton, C.E. (1967) "Artifical and Natural Languages." In P. Edwards (ed.), *The Encyclopedia of Philosophy*, vol. 1. New York: Macmillan Co. and The Free Press, pp. 168–171.

Chambers, R. (1844) *Vestiges of the National History of Creation*. London: Churchill.

Chisholm, R. (1946) "The Contrary to Fact Conditional," *Mind* 55: 289–307.

Copi, I. (1967) *Symbolic Logic*, 3rd ed. New York: Macmillan Co.

Dawkins, R. (1982) *The Extended Phenotype: The Gene as the Unit of Selection*. San Francisco: Freeman.

Darwin, C. (1968) *The Origin of Species*, 1st ed., edited by J.W. Burrow. Harmondsworth, Eng.: Penguin Books.

Diederich, W. (1982) "Review Article: Stegmuller on the Stucturalist Approach in the Philosophy of Science," *Erkenntnis* 17: 377–397.

Dobzhansky, Th. (1951) *Genetics and the Origin of Species*, 3rd ed. New York: Columbia University Press.

Dray, W. (1957) *Laws and Explanation in History*. Oxford: Oxford University Press.

Eldredge, N. (1985a) *Time Frames: The Rethinking of Darwinian Evolution and the Theory of Punctuated Equilibria*. New York: Simon and Schuster.

_____ . (1985b) *The Unifinished Synthesis: Biological Hierarchies and Modern Evolutionary Thought*. New York: Oxford University Press.

Eldredge, N. and Gould, S.J. (1972) "Punctuated Equilibria: An Alternative to Phyletic Gradualism." In T.M.J. Schopf (ed.), *Models in Paleobiology*. San Francisco: Freeman.

Feigl, H. (1970) "The 'Orthodox' View of Theories: Remarks in Defence as Well as Critique." In M. Radner and S. Winokur. (eds.), *Minnesota Studies in the Philosophy of Science*, vol. 4. Minneapolis: University of Minnesota Press, pp. 3–16.

Feyerbend, P. (1965) "On the Meaning of Scientific Terms," *Journal of Philosophy* 62: 266–274.

Fisher, R.A. (1950) *The Genetical Theory of Natural Selection*. Oxford: Clarendon Press.

Gallie, W.B. (1955) "Explanation in History and the Genetic Sciences," *Mind* 64: 160–180.

Giere, R.N. (1976) "A Laplacean Formal Semantics for Single Case Propensities," *Journal of Philosophical Logic* 5: 321–353.

_____ . (1977) "Testing *vs.* Information Models of Statistical Inference." In

R.G. Colodny (ed.), *Logic, Laws and Life*. Pittsburg: University of Pittsburg Press, pp. 19–70.

———. (1979) *Understanding Scientific Reasoning*. New York: Holt, Reinhart and Winston.

———. (1983) "Testing Theoretical Hypotheses." In J. Earman (ed.), Minnesota Studies in the Philosophy of Science, vol. 10, *Testing Scientific Theories*. Minneapolis: University of Minnesota Press, pp. 269–298.

Ginsburg, S. (1960) "Some Remarks on Abstract Machines," *Transaction of the American Mathematical Society* 96: 400–444.

Goodman, N. (1947) "The Problem of Counterfactual Conditionals," *Journal of Philosophy* 44: 113–128.

Goudge, T. (1961) *The Ascent of Life*. Toronto: University of Toronto Press.

Gould, S.J. (1976) "Biological Potential *vs* Biological Determinism," *Natural History Magazine* 85: 12–22.

———. (1978) "Sociobiology: The Art of Storytelling," *New Scientist* 80 (Nov. 16): 530–533.

———. (1980a) "The Promise of Paleobiology as a Nomothetic Evolutionary Discipline," *Paleobiology* 6: 96–118.

———. (1980b) "Is a New and General Theory of Evolution Emerging?" *Paleobiology* 6: 119–130.

———. (1981) "But Not Wright Enough: A Reply to Orzack," *Paleobiology* 7: 128–131.

———. (1982) "Darwinism and the Expansion of Evolutioanry Theory," *Science* 216: 380–387.

Gould, S.J., and Eldredge, N. (1977) "Punctuated Equilibria: The Tempo and Mode of Evolution Reconsidered," *Paleobiology* 3: 115–151.

Hanson, N.R. (1958) *Patterns of Discovery*. Cambridge: Cambridge University Press.

———. (1969a) *Perception and Discovery: An Introduction to Scientific Inquiry*. San Francisco: Freeman.

———. (1969b) "Logical Positivism and the Interpretation of Scientific Theories." In P. Achinstein and S. Barker (eds.), *The Legacy of Logical Positivism*. Baltimore, Md.: Johns Hopkins Press, pp. 57–84.

Hempel. C. (1965) *Aspects of Scientific Explanation*. New York: The Free Press.

———. (1967) *Philosophy of Natural Science*. Englewood Cliffs, N.J.: Prentice-Hall.

Hempel, C., and Oppenheim, P. (1948) "Studies in the Logic of Explanation," *Philosophy of Science* 15: 135–175.

Hilbert, D. (1902) *The Foundations of Geometry*, translated by E.J. Townsend. Chicago: Open Court.

Hull, D.L. (1972) "Reduction in Genetics—Biology or Philosophy?" *Philosophy of Science* 39: 491–499.

———. (1973) "Reduction in Genetics—Doing the Impossible." In P. Suppes et al. (eds.), *Logic, Methodology and Philosophy of Science*, vol. 4. Amsterdam: North Holland, pp. 619–635.

———. (1974) *Philosophy of Biological Science*. Englewood Cliffs, N.J.: Prentice-Hall.

———. (1976) "Informal Aspects of Theory Reduction." In R.S. Cohen et al. (eds.), *PSA 1974*. Dordrecht: Reidel, pp. 653–670.

———. (1979) "Discussion: Reduction in Genetics," *Philosophy of Science* 46: 316–320.

———. (1980) "Individuality and Selection," *Annual Review of Ecology and Systematics* 11: 311–332.

———.(1982) "The Naked Meme," In H.C. Plotkin (ed.), *Learning, Development and Culture: Essays in Evolutionary Epistemology*. Chichester: Wiley, pp. 273–327.

———. (1983) "Exemplars and Scientific Change." In P.D. Asquith and R. Nickles (eds.), *PSA 1982*, vol. 2. East Lansing, Mich.: Philosophy of Science Association, pp. 479–503.

———. (1985) "Darwinism as a Historical Entity: A Historiographic Proposal." In D. Kohn (ed.), *The Darwinian Heritage*. Princeton, N.J.: Princeton University Press, pp. 773–812.

———. (1988a) "A Mechanism and Its Metaphysics: An Evolutionary Account of the Social and Conceptual Development of Science," *Biology and Philosophy*, vol. 3.

———. (1988b) *Science as a Process: An Evolutionary Account of the*

Social and Conceptual Development of Science. Chicago: University of Chicago Press.

Hunter, G. (1971) *Metalogic: An Introduction to the Metatheory of Standard First-Order Logic*. London: Macmillan Co.

Kaplansky, I. (1977) *Set Theory and Metric Spaces*. Boston: Allyn and Bacon.

Kuhn, T.S. (1962) *The Structure of Scientific Revolutions*. Chicago: Chicago University Press.

_____ . (1970) "Reflections on My Critics." In I Lakatos and A. Musgrave (eds.), *Criticism and the Growth of Knowledge*. Cambridge: Cambridge University Press, pp. 231–278.

Kimura, M. (1983) *The Neutral Theory of Molecular Evolution*. Cambridge: Cambridge University Press.

Kuratowski, K. (1972) *Introduction to Set Theory and Topology*, 2nd ed. New York: Pergamon Press.

Kyburg, H.J. Jr. (1968) *Philosophy of Science: A Formal Approach*. New York: MacMillan Co.

Lack, D. (1947) *Darwin's Finches: An Essay on the General Biological Theory of Evolution*. Cambridge: Cambridge University Press.

Lamark, J.B. (1809) *Philosophie Zoologique*. London: Macmillan, 1914 (rpt.).

Lewontin, R. (1974) *The Genetic Basis of Evolutionary Change*. Columbia: Columbia University Press.

_____ . (1977) "Sociobiology: A Caricature of Darwinism." In F. Suppe and P.D. Asquith (eds.), *PSA 1976*, vol. 2. East Lansing, Mich.: Philosophy of Science Association, pp. 22–31.

_____ . (1980) "Theoretical Population Genetics in the Evolutionary Synthesis." In E. Mayr and W.B. Provine (eds.), *The Evolutionary Synthesis*. Cambridge, Mass.: Harvard University Press.

Lloyd, E. (1983) "The Nature of Darwin's Support for the Theory of Natural Selection," *Philosophy of Science* 50: 112–129.

_____ . (1984) "A Semantic Approach to the Structure of Population Genetics," *Philosophy of Science* 51: 242–264.

_____ . (1986) "Thinking about Models in Evolutionary Theory," *Philosophica* 37: 87–100.

———— . (1987) "Confirmation of Ecological and Evolutionary Models," *Biology and Philosophy* 2: 277–293.

———— . (In Press) *The Structure of Confirmation of Evolutionary Theory.*

Lumsden, C., and Gushurst, A.C. (1985) "Gene-Culture Coevolution: Humankind in the Making." In J.H. Fetzer (ed.), *Sociobiology and Epistemology*, Dordrecht: Reidel, pp. 3–28.

Lumsden, C., and Wilson, E.O. (1981) *Genes, Mind and Culture*. Cambridge, Mass.: Harvard University Press.

———— . (1983) *Promethean Fire*. Cambridge, Mass.: Harvard University Press.

Mackie, J.L. (1977) *Ethics: Inventing Right and Wrong*. Harmondsworth, Eng.: Penguin Books.

Mayr, E. (1963) *Animal Species and Evolution* Cambridge, Mass.: Belknap.

Montagu, A. (ed.) (1980) *Sociobiology Examined.*Oxford: Oxford University Press.

Moore, G.E. (1903) *Principia Ethica*. Cambridge: Cambridge University Press.

Moore-Ede, M.C., et al., (1982)*The Clocks that Time Us: Physiology of the Circadian Timing System*. Cambridge, Mass.: Harvard University Press.

Nagel, E. (1961) *The Structure of Science*. New York: Harcourt, Brace.

Nagel, E. and Newman, J.R. (1968) *Godel's Proof*. New York: New York University Press.

Nagel, E., Suppes, P., and Tarski, A. (eds.) (1962) *Logic, Methodology and Philosophy of Sciency: Proceedings of the 1960 International Congress*. Stanford, Calif.: Stanford University Press, pp. 252–261.

Newton-Smith, W.H. (1981) *The Rationality of Science*. Boston: Routledge & Kegan Paul.

Orzack, S.H. (1981) "The Modern Synthesis is Partly Wright," *Paleobiology* 7: 131–134.

Peters, R. (1959) "Observationalism in Psychology," *Mind* 68: ???.

Pinter, C.C. (1971) *Set Theory*. Reading, Mass.: Addison-Wesley.

Plotkin, H.C., and Odling-Smee, F.J. (1981) "A Multiple-level Model of

Evolution and Its Implications for Sociobiology," *Behavior and Brain Science* 4: 225–268.

Popper, K. (1959) *The Logic of Scientific Discovery.* London: Hutchinson & Co. Ltd.

———. (1965) *Conjectures and Refutations: The Growth of Scientific Knowledge*, 2nd ed. New York: Basic Books.

Putnam, H. (1962) "What Theories Are Not." In E. Nagel, P. Suppes, and A. Tarski (eds.), *Logic, Methodology and Philosophy of Science.* Stanford, Calif: Stanford University Press, pp. 240–251.

Quine, W.V.O. (1951) "Two Dogmas of Empiricism," *Philosophical Review* 60: 20–43.

Richerson, P.J., and Boyd, R. (1978) "A Dual Inheritance Model of the Human Evolutionary Process I: Basic Postulates and Simple Model," *Journal of Social and Biological Structures* 1: 127–154.

Rosenberg, A. (1980) "Ruse's Treatment of the Evidence for Evolution: A Reconsideration." In P.D. Asquith and R.N. Giere (eds.), *PSA 1980*, vol. 1. East Lansing, Mich.: Philosophy of Science Association.

———. (1981) "The Interaction of Evolutionary and Genetic Theory." In L.W. Sumner, J.G. Slater, and F.F. Wilson (eds.), *Pragmatism and Purpose: Essays Presented to Thomas Goudge.* Toronto: University of Toronto Press.

———. (1985) *The Structure of Biological Science.* Cambridge: Cambridge University Press.

Rosenberg, A., and Williams, M. (1986) "Discussion: Fitness as Primitive and Propensity," *Philosophy of Science* 53: 412–418.

Ruse, M. (1971) "Reduction, Replacement and Molecular Biology," *Dialectica* 25: 1–38.

———. (1973) *The Philosophy of Biology.* London: Hutchinson & Co. Ltd.

———. (1975) "Charles Darwin's Theory of Evolution: An Analysis," *Journal of the History of Biology* 8: 219–241.

———. (1976) "Reduction in Genetics." In R.S. Cohen et al. (eds.), *PSA 1974*, Dordrecht: Reidel, pp. 633–651.

———. (1977b) "Sociobiology: Sound Science or Muddled Metaphysics?" In F. Suppe and P.D. Asquith (eds.), *PSA 1976*, vol. 2. East Lansing, Mich.: Philosophy of Science Assocaiton, pp. 48–73.

_____. (1979a) *The Darwinian Revolution: Science Red in Tooth and Claw*. Chicago: University of Chicago Press.

_____. (1979b) *Sociobiology: Sense or Nonsense?* Dordrecht: Reidel.

_____. (1982) *Darwinism Defended: A Guide to the Evolution Controversies*. Reading, Mass: Addison-Wesley.

_____. (1986) *Taking Darwin Seriously*. Oxford: Basil Blackwell.

Ruse, M., and Wilson, E.O. (1986) "Ethics as Applied Science," *Philosophy* 173–192.

Sahlins, M.D. (1976) *The Use and Abuse of Biology*, Ann Arbor, Mich.: University of Michigan Press.

Saunders, D.S. d(1977)] *An Introduction to Biological Rhythms*. Glasgow: Blackie.

Schaffner, K.F. (1969) "Correspondence Rules," *Philosophy of Science* 36: 280–290.

Scriven, M. (1958) "Definitions, Explanations, and Theories." In H. Feigl, M. Scriven, and G. Maxwell (eds.), *Minnesota Studies in the Philosophy of Science*, vol. 2. Minneapolis: University of Minnesota Press.

_____. (1959a) "Explanation and Prediction in Evolutionary Theory," *Science* 130: 477–482.

_____. (1959b) "Truisms as the Grounds for Historical Explanations." In P. Gardiner (ed.), *Theories of History*, New York: The Free Press.

_____. (1961) "The Key Property of Physical Laws-Inaccuracy." In *Current Issues in the Philosophy of Science* H. Feigl and G. Maxwell (eds.), New York: Holt, Rinehart and Winston.

_____. (1962) "Explanations, Predictions, and Laws." In H. Feigl and G. Maxwell (eds.), *Minnesota Studies in the Philosophy of Science*, vol. 3. Minneapolis: University of Minnesota Press.

Simon, M. (1971) *The Matter of Life*. New Haven, Conn.: Yale University Press.

Simpson, G.G. (1953) *The Major Features of Evolution*. New York: Columbia University Press.

Skinner, B.F. (1945) "The Operationalist Analysis of Psychological Terms," *Psychological Review* 52: 270–277.

Sneed, J. (1971) *The Logical Structure of Mathematical Physics*. Dordrecht: Reidel.

Sober, E. (1981) "Holism, Individualism, and the Units of Selection." In P.D. Asquith and R.N. Giere, (eds.), *PSA 1980*, vol. 2. East Lansing, Mich.: Philosophy of Science Association, pp. 93–121.

_____ . (1984a) "Fact, Fiction, and Fitness: A Reply to Rosenberg," *Journal of Philosophy* 81: 372–383.

_____ . (1984b) *The Nature of Selection*. Cambridge, Mass.: MIT Press.

_____ . (In press) "What is Evolutionary Altruism," *Canadian Journal of Philosophy*.

Sober, E., and Lewontin, R.C. (1982) "Artifact, Cause, and Genic Selection," *Philosophy of Science* 49: 157–180.

Stebbins, G.L., and Ayala, F.J. (1981) "Is a New Evolutionary Synthesis Necessary?" *Science* 213: 967–971.

Stegmuller, W. (1976) *The Structure and Dynamics of Theories*. New York: Springer-Verlag.

Stevens, S.S. (1935a) "The Operaitonal Basis of Psychology," *American Journal of Psychology* 46: 323–330.

_____ . (1935b) "The Operational Definition of Psychological Concepts," *Psychological Review* 42: 517–527.

Stoll, R.R. (1963) *Set Theory and Logic*. San Francisco: W.H. Freeman and Co.

Suppe, F. (1967) *On the Meaning and Use of Models in Mathematics and the Exact Sciences*. Ann Arbor, Mich.: University Microfilms International (Ph.D. Dissertation).

_____ . (1972a) "Theories, Their Formulations, and the Operational Imperative," *Synthese* 25: 129–164.

_____ . (1972b) "What's Wrong With the Received View on the Structure of Scientific Theories?" *Philosophy of Science* 39: 1–19.

_____ . (1974) "Theories and Phenomena." In W. Leinfellner and E. Kohler (eds.), *Developments in the Methodology of Social Science*. Dordrecht: Reidel, pp. 45–91.

_____ . (1976) "Theoretical Laws." In M. Prezlecki, K. Szaniawski, and R.

Wojcicki (ed.), *Formal Method in the Methodology of Empirical Science*. Wroclaw: Ossolineum.

_____ . (1977) *The Structure of Scientific Theories* 2nd ed. Urbana: The University of Illinois Press.

_____ . (1979) "Theory Structure." In P.D. Asquith and H.E. Kyburg, Jr. (eds.), *Current Research in the Philosophy of Science*, East Lansing, Mich.: Philosophy of Science Association.

_____ . (In press) *The Semantic Conception of Theories and Scientific Realism*. Urbana: University of Illinois Press.

Suppes, P. (1957) *Introduction to Logic*. Princeton, N.J.: Van Nostrand.

_____ . (1962) "Models of Data." In E. Nagel, P. Suppes, and A. Tarski (eds.), *Logic, Methodology and Philosophy of Science*. Stanford, Calif.: Stanford University Press, pp. 252–261.

_____ . (1967) "What is a Scientific Theory?" In S. Morgenbesser (ed.), *Philosophy of Science Today*. New York: Basic Books, pp. 55–67.

_____ . (1968) "The Desirability of Formalization in Science," *Journal of Philosophy* 65: 651–664.

Taylor, C. (1964) *The Explanation of Behaviour*. New York: Humanities Press.

Thagard, P. (1981) "Critical Notice of Michael Ruse, *Sociobiology: Sense or Nonsense?*" *Canadian Journal of Philosophy* 11: 751–759.

Thompson, P. (1980) "Is Sociobiology a Pseudoscience?" In P.D. Asquith and R.N. Giere (eds.), *PSA 1980*, vol. 1. East Lansing, Mich.: Philosophy of Science Association.

_____ . (1983a) "Tempo and Mode in Evolution: Punctuated Equilibria and the Modern Synthetic Theory," *Philosophy of Science* 50: 432–452.

_____ . (1983b) "The Structure of Evolutionary Theory: A Semantic Approach," *Studies in History and Philosophy of Science* 14: 215–229.

_____ . (1983c) "Historical Laws in Modern Biology," *Acta Biotheoretica* 32: 167–177.

_____ . (1985) "Sociobiological Explanation and the Testability of Sociobiological Theory." In J.H. Fetzer (ed.), *Sociobiology and Epistemology*. Dordrecht: Reidel, pp. 201–215.

_____ . (1986) "The Interaction of Theories and the Semantic Conception of Evolutionary Theory," *Philosophica* 37: 73–86.

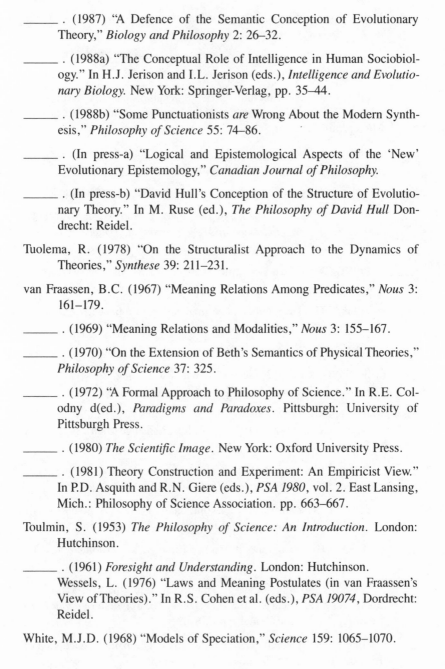

_____ . (1987) "A Defence of the Semantic Conception of Evolutionary Theory," *Biology and Philosophy* 2: 26–32.

_____ . (1988a) "The Conceptual Role of Intelligence in Human Sociobiology." In H.J. Jerison and I.L. Jerison (eds.), *Intelligence and Evolutionary Biology*. New York: Springer-Verlag, pp. 35–44.

_____ . (1988b) "Some Punctuationists *are* Wrong About the Modern Synthesis," *Philosophy of Science* 55: 74–86.

_____ . (In press-a) "Logical and Epistemological Aspects of the 'New' Evolutionary Epistemology," *Canadian Journal of Philosophy*.

_____ . (In press-b) "David Hull's Conception of the Structure of Evolutionary Theory." In M. Ruse (ed.), *The Philosophy of David Hull* Dondrecht: Reidel.

Tuolema, R. (1978) "On the Structuralist Approach to the Dynamics of Theories," *Synthese* 39: 211–231.

van Fraassen, B.C. (1967) "Meaning Relations Among Predicates," *Nous* 3: 161–179.

_____ . (1969) "Meaning Relations and Modalities," *Nous* 3: 155–167.

_____ . (1970) "On the Extension of Beth's Semantics of Physical Theories," *Philosophy of Science* 37: 325.

_____ . (1972) "A Formal Approach to Philosophy of Science." In R.E. Colodny d(ed.), *Paradigms and Paradoxes*. Pittsburgh: University of Pittsburgh Press.

_____ . (1980) *The Scientific Image*. New York: Oxford University Press.

_____ . (1981) Theory Construction and Experiment: An Empiricist View." In P.D. Asquith and R.N. Giere (eds.), *PSA 1980*, vol. 2. East Lansing, Mich.: Philosophy of Science Association. pp. 663–667.

Toulmin, S. (1953) *The Philosophy of Science: An Introduction*. London: Hutchinson.

_____ . (1961) *Foresight and Understanding*. London: Hutchinson.
Wessels, L. (1976) "Laws and Meaning Postulates (in van Fraassen's View of Theories)." In R.S. Cohen et al. (eds.), *PSA 19074*, Dordrecht: Reidel.

White, M.J.D. (1968) "Models of Speciation," *Science* 159: 1065–1070.

Wilder, R.L. (1965) *The Foundations of Mathematics*, 2nd ed. New York: John Wiley and Sons.

Williams, M.B. (1970) "Deducing the Consequences of Evolution," *Journal of Theoretical Biology*, 29: 343–385.

_____ . (1973a) "Falsifiable Predictions of Evolutionary Theory," *Philosophy of Science* 40: 518–537.

_____ . (1973b) "The Logical Status of Natural Selection and Other Evolutionary Controversies." In M. Bunge (ed.), *The Methodological Unity of Science*. Dordrecht: Reidel.

_____ . (1982) "The Importance of Prediction Testing in Evolutionary Biology," *Erkenntnis* 17: 291–306.

Wilson, E.O. (1975) *Sociobiology: The New Synthesis*. Cambridge: Belknap Press.

Wilson, F.F. (1968a) "A Note on Operationism," *Critica* 2: 79–87

(1968b) "Is Operationism Unjust to Temperature?" *Synthese* 18: 394–422.

(1985) *Explanation, Causation and Deduction*. Dordrecht: Reidel.

Woodger, J.H. (1929) *Biological Principles: A Critical Study*. London: Routledge and Kegan Paul.

_____ . (1937) *The Axiomatic Method in Biology*. Cambridge: Cambridge University Press.

_____ . (1939) *The Technique of Theory Construction*. Chicago: University of Chicago Press.

_____ . (1952) *Biology and Language*, Cambridge: Cambridge University Press.

Worrall, J. (1984) "Review Article: An Unreal Image," *British Journal for the Philosophy of Science* 35: 65–80.

Index

145

Fairleigh Dickinson University Library
Teaneck, New Jersey

T001-15M
3-15-71